Angler's Mail

COARSE FISHING YEAR

Angler's Mail

COARSE FISHING YEAR

WITH DAVE COSTER, TONY WHIELDON AND ROY WESTWOOD

THE STORM'S OVER AS QUICKLY AS IT BEGAN— BACK TO A BLACK TIP ON THE FLOAT AND I'M INTO A BETTER FISH STRAIGHT AWAY.

CLB

Colour Library Books

CONTENTS

CLB 2851
This edition published by Colour Library Books Ltd,
Godalming, Surrey, GU7 1XW
Copyright © The Hamlyn Publishing Group Limited 1990

ISBN 0 86283 881 9

Produced by Mandarin Offset
Printed in Hong Kong

THE APPEARANCE OF THE PERCH IS FOLLOWED BY A STRANGE LULL — I WONDER WHAT'S HAPPENED TO THE CHUB?

Tony Whieldon

INTRODUCTION

Below: Dave Coster
Right: Tony Whieldon
Below right: Roy Westwood

Within weeks of its debut in the centre pages of *Angler's Mail*, we knew the Fishing Diary colour strip was destined to become a classic series that would run and run.

It offered everything the modern coarse angler wanted from pure and basic instruction to advanced techniques – and all graphically presented in a no-nonsense style that is instantly understandable.

Now the most memorable of those diaries recording the weekly adventures of tackle dealer Dave Coster have been collected together in this unique edition embracing the whole fishing year.

I'm aware that many thousands of Fishing Diary addicts are intrigued to know if the storylines are actually true or simply wishful thinking. They also wonder how artist Tony Whieldon manages to accurately paint every blade of grass in favourite swims from Perth to Exeter!

This is the right moment to spill the beans. There is nothing fictional about the Fishing Diary – the ups and downs during Dave's weekly Diary trips are honestly documented at the time. I should know because I shadow him with my cameras when I'm not actually fishing by his side. After every session, Dave writes up the diary with accompanying sketches and these are then expanded on with a series of colour prints capturing the most significant moments of the day.

Dave's swim is photographed from every conceivable angle and it's this comprehensive package of words, pictures and sketches on which Tony Whieldon sets to work in his Devon studio to portray his own evocative interpretation. So now you know – each and every adventure actually happened just as it has been illustrated by Tony Whieldon!

I'm confident you will find this book highly entertaining but I urge you to study the technical instruction and shrewd tactical thinking that's handed out by Dave along the way. He has got one of the sharpest fishing brains of his generation and continually amazes with his ability to recognise the correct feeding and presentation methods on whichever bank he plants his tackle box.

In fact, Dave has never failed to net a fish and learn a lesson or two in scores of expeditions and that is remarkable considering some of the hostile weather and river conditions we have endured. His flair always saves the day.

On behalf of Dave and Tony, I would like to thank all those fishery owners, specimen hunters and matchmen who have played their part in making the *Angler's Mail* Fishing Diary series a fascinating work of art.

ROY WESTWOOD

Editor, *Angler's Mail*

JANUARY
River Kennet
Newbury, Berkshire

SHALLOWS
SHALLOWS (TROUT)
ISLAND
SHALLOWS
FOOTBRIDGE

SPECIALIST ANGLER BOB JAMES HAS OFFERED ME THE RARE CHANCE TO FISH A PRIVATE TROUT BEAT ON THE BERKSHIRE KENNET. THERE'S BIG ROACH, CHUB, DACE AND GRAYLING — I CAN'T WAIT TO GET STARTED.

BOB JAMES

BOB'S END RIG FOR FISHING BREAD ON THE HOOK WITH A 2/3 MASHED BREAD AND 1/3 MASTERCLASS FEEDBAIT MIX IN THE TINY FEEDER.

PEG LEG STOP
3.5lb ULTIMA
3ft
SWAN SHOT
18in
SMALL CUT DOWN DRENNAN FEEDER
SIZE B SEALEY OCTOPUS MATCH HOOK

ISOTOPE

SHIMANO CUSTOM GTM 2500
ROD
QUIVERTIP
NORMAL TIP

BOB'S RODS ARE FASCINATING. HE USES FLY FISHING BLANKS SPECIALLY ADAPTED FOR BIG ROACH FISHING. KENT CARPMAN MIKE HARRIS MADE UP THESE RODS AND SPECIAL QUIVER-TIPS. THE VERY SOFT BLANKS PREVENT BIG ROACH FROM ROLLING OFF THE HOOK.

BOB TRIES BOTH SIDES OF THE WEED RACK WITH HIS BREAD BAITS BUT THE CHUB ARE STRANGELY SULLEN. HE WANDERS BACK UPSTREAM TO ANOTHER RACK CONSTRUCTED FROM SCAFFOLDING POLES AND IMMEDIATELY HOOKS INTO A SMALL GRAYLING.

IT SEEMS THE GRAYLING HAVE SHOALED UP IN THE FAST WATER SURGING THROUGH THE RACK WHICH LIES AT THE BACK OF AN ISLAND. *THE ACTION IS FAST AND FURIOUS.*

I'VE STOPPED OFF ABOVE THIS CARRIER WHICH RUNS UNDER THE MAIN KENNET. BOB TELLS ME THE FISH LIE UP JUST BEYOND THE HUMP IN THE RIVERBED CAUSED BY THE CULVERT ROOF.

LOOSE FEEDING SHOULD DRAW THEM UP WITHIN RANGE OF THE STICK FLOAT.

MEANWHILE BOB'S SET UP TWO RODS JUST ABOVE THE WEED RACK. HE'S HOPING FOR BIG CHUB WHICH USUALLY RESPOND PRETTY QUICKLY TO BREAD BAITS. THERE'S A MASSIVE PIKE ESTIMATED AT 30lb IN THE SLACK — THAT COULD SPELL TROUBLE.

I'VE BEEN FISHING FOR AN HOUR WITHOUT A BITE WHEN SUDDENLY I PULLED OUT A DACE. NEXT CAST I HOOK SOMETHING BETTER.

A LOVELY 2lb RAINBOW TROUT — LET'S PUT HIM STRAIGHT BACK.

AFTER HOOKING OUT SEVERAL GRAYLING BOB RECOMMENDS I HAVE A GO AS WELL IN THE FAST WATER. WALKING BACK UPSTREAM TOWARDS THE ISLAND I FIND DRAMATIC EVIDENCE OF THE POTENTIAL DROUGHT CRISIS FACING OUR RIVERS. THIS MUDFLAT SHOULD BE COVERED BY WATER AT THIS TIME OF YEAR BUT THE FLOW IS <u>BELOW</u> SUMMER LEVEL. MAKES ME WONDER IF THE ROACH WILL SHOW TODAY.

River Kennet Continued

● Private stretches of water are not necessarily superior to club or day ticket fisheries. This is certainly true on the Kennet where several of the more prolific barbel lengths are accessible on local club cards.

I'M STUCK INTO A SHOAL OF GRAYLING ON A PRIVATE STRETCH OF THE KENNET. THIS IS MY FOURTEENTH IN TWENTY MINUTES.

ALMOST AS THOUGH THEY KNOW THE PIKE HAS HAD ITS FILL THE CHUB START TO MOVE ON BOB'S BREAD FEED AND AS THE LIGHT FADES HE STARTS TO GET A FEW INDICATIONS.

HE WAS JUST GETTING THE BETTER OF THE FISH WHEN A 30lb PIKE DASHED THROUGH THE RACK AND GRABBED IT! BOB FELT HIS LINE GRATING AGAINST THE WOODEN SUPPORTS AS THE PIKE MOVED BACK INTO ITS LAIR. THE ODDS WERE HOPELESS AND BOB TELLS ME IT'S THE SECOND BIG CHUB HE'S LOST TO THE SAME PIKE THIS SEASON.

THE BEST OF THE DAY AT NEARLY 2lb.

NOW THE LIGHT'S FAILING I'M GOING TO SWITCH TO BREAD ON THIS LIGHT BOMB RIG I'VE BEEN EXPERIMENTING WITH RECENTLY.

2.5lb

STAND-OFF LOOP KNOT

1.7lb HOOKLENGTH

Nº 12 GAMAKATSU SILVER MICROBARB

⅛oz BOMB

TWISTED LINK KEEPS HOOKLENGTH CLEAR

I CAN SEE WHAT BOB MEANS. THAT WAS THE TINIEST OF MOVEMENTS, ALMOST COULD HAVE BEEN WEED BRUSHING THE LINE BUT IT WASN'T.

IT'S A 12oz DACE.

IT'S GETTING VERY DARK NOW. I WAS REALLY HOPING FOR ONE OF THE KENNET'S BIG ROACH — IF YOU'RE GOING TO GET ONE NOW'S THE TIME.

MEANWHILE BOB JAMES HAS RETURNED TO HIS WEED RACK SWIM ON THE BOTTOM BOUNDARY AND HITS INTO A GOOD CHUB ON BREAD. LOOKS ALL OF 4lb.

I'VE MOVED BACK DOWNSTREAM TO A KNOWN BIG ROACH SWIM WHERE I'LL TRY TROTTING BREADFLAKE AND FEEDING MASHED BREAD.

I HOOK A BIG FISH IMMEDIATELY BUT IT RUNS INTO A SNAG AND I LOSE IT.

NEXT CAST I'M INTO ANOTHER POWERFUL FISH — A NICE GRAYLING...

BOB'S HIT ONE OF THE TINY MOVEMENTS ON HIS FINE QUIVERTIP AND A GOOD FISH IS ON.

A 4lb PLUS CHUB IS DRAWN AWAY FROM THE RACK AND INTO HIS NET.

YES! AGAIN IT WAS THE TINIEST OF TOUCHES BUT I'VE CONNECTED.

MY PERSEVERANCE HAS BEEN REWARDED WITH A PERFECT 2lb ROACH — 1/2 AN OUNCE OVER THE MAGIC BARRIER IN FACT. EVEN BETTER THAN WINNING A MATCH!

THAT ROGUE PIKE RATHER DESTROYED BOB'S PLANS. ALTHOUGH HE'S BETTER KNOWN AS A CARP ANGLER HE'S NO STRANGER TO BIG ROACH. HE DIDN'T GET ONE TODAY BUT HE'S JUST AS DELIGHTED THAT I DID. THANK'S MATE.

JANUARY
Salmonhutch Lakes
Crediton, Devon

SPRINGS

DAVE'S THIRD SWIM

DAVE'S SECOND SWIM

TONY'S SWIM

DAVE'S FIRST SWIM

WIND

OUTLET

RIVER YEO

THESE THREE POOLS USED TO BE ONE LAKE WHICH AT ONE TIME HELD LARGE PERCH, ROACH AND SHOALS' OF DACE. THE LAKE WAS DRAINED AND EXCAVATED TO FORM ITS PRESENT SHAPE.

TONY WHIELDON, WHO FISHED HERE AS A BOY, HAS TUCKED HIMSELF AWAY IN THE TOP CORNER OF THE MIDDLE POOL. A LOT OF THOUGHT HAS GONE INTO THIS FISHERY— IT'S NICE TO SEE FEATURES CREATED RATHER THAN JUST A DUG HOLE WITH AS MANY SWIMS AS POSSIBLE CRAMMED IN.

I'VE SPENT AN HOUR FISHING THE DEEPER WATER OFF THE ISLAND WITHOUT A BITE — I'M NOW WORKING MY TACKLE UP THE SHELF INTO THE SHALLOWS TO SEE IF THERE'S ANYTHING ABOUT.

MEANWHILE TONY HAS HIT INTO HIS FIRST FISH ON SWEETCORN.

SOON AFTER, A SWITCH TO CRUST STARTS BRINGING GOOD TAKES.

TONY'S STRUCK INTO ANOTHER, BETTER FISH, SO I'VE MOVED UP TO SEE IF I CAN JOIN IN THE ACTION — THIS IS AMAZING! I'VE PUT IN LOADS OF CASTERS AND YET CAN'T BUY A BITE. TONY IS FISHING MUCH CRUDER AND IS STILL GETTING TAKES. THE FISH HERE JUST DON'T WANT TO KNOW MY MATCH APPROACH.

I'M GOING TO START ON THE FIRST POOL. THERE ARE CARP MOVING JUST PAST THE POINT OF THAT ISLAND. EACH POOL WAS STOCKED WITH CARP ABOUT 18 MONTHS AGO, SOME INTO DOUBLE FIGURES. TENCH WERE ALSO STOCKED INTO THE TOP POOL.

IT'S A FULLY SCALED MIRROR CARP OF 5 lb.

DAVE COSTER'S RIG   TONY WHIELDON'S RIG

INSERT WAGGLER

STUMPY WAGGLER

RUBBER TUBING

SSG   AAA

LOOSE CASTERS

LOOSE SWEETCORN

No. 8

ALTERNATING CRUST AND SWEETCORN

2 AAA

No. 10

No. 4

1·7 lb HOOKLENGTH

DOUBLE CASTER

IT'S JUST NOT MY DAY! THERE WAS A BAD SNAG IN MY LAST SWIM SO I'VE NOW MOVED FOR A THIRD TIME TO THE TOP LAKE. TONY'S GONE STALKING SOME FISH HE'S SEEN MOVING AT THE BOTTOM OF THE MIDDLE POOL. I'M NOW FEEDING TWO LINES, PUTTING CASTERS ACROSS TO THOSE TREES AND SWEETCORN JUST OVER THE NEARSIDE RUSHES...

...THAT'S MORE LIKE IT— A BITE FIRST CAST WHICH TOOK ME BY SURPRISE AND I MISSED IT, BUT IT'S A GOOD SIGN.

I THINK THERE'S A REAL CHANCE AT LAST OF BREAKING MY DUCK...

Salmonhutch Lakes Continued

● There's no Close Season for coarse fishing on Devon stillwaters and many of them remain open all year round. According to fishery owners, this does not appear to affect the well being of the fish or standard of sport.

AFTER MISSING MY FIRST BITE IN THIS SWIM ON THE TOP LAKE AT SALMONHUTCH I'M STRUGGLING AGAIN.

...BUT TONY WHIELDON HAS FOUND

THE FISH GAVE A GOOD ACCOUNT OF ITSELF AND TURNS OUT TO BE THE BEST OF THE DAY AT 7lb — THE SMALL CARP THAT WENT INTO THESE POOLS ARE PUTTING ON WEIGHT FAST.

I DON'T BELIEVE IT — THE HOOK'S PULLED FREE AT THE NET!

TONY'S TAKEN HALF A DOZEN CARP NOW BY STALKING. IT'S NOT REALLY MY STYLE, BUT I THINK I'LL HAVE A GO, AS MY SWIM'S DRIED UP.

CARP AGAIN AFTER LEAVING HIS TACKLE AND GOING STALKING

AT LAST! A GOOD BITE AND I'VE GOT A FISH ON!

AFTER ANOTHER LONG WAIT I GET ANOTHER SAILAWAY BITE AND LAND MY FIRST FISH.

I HAD TO SWITCH TO SWEETCORN TO DO IT — I STILL CAN'T BUY A BITE ON CASTER OR MAGGOT.

MEANWHILE ANOTHER YOUNG ANGLER HAS CAUGHT A HUGE MINNOW! THE BRITISH RECORD IS LESS THAN 1oz — THE FISH HERE MUST AVERAGE THAT.

THAT'S AMAZING! FIRST CAST AND A 3lb CARP HAS SNATCHED MY SWEETCORN ON-THE-DROP!

TONY ENDED UP WITH SEVEN FISH TO 7lb, I JUST HAD THE TWO. I THINK ONCE SOME BAIT GOES IN, MY APPROACH WILL ACCOUNT FOR SOME BIG CATCHES. ONCE A FEW EXTRA SPECIES ARE STOCKED TO GIVE MORE VARIATION SALMONHUTCH WILL BECOME A CLASS FISHERY.

IT'S A LONG DRIVE ACROSS COUNTRY TO DEVON — BUT CARP LIKE THESE ARE CERTAINLY WORTH THE PETROL.

FEBRUARY
Perth Harbour
River Tay, Perthshire

I'M OVER 400 MILES AWAY FROM HOME TODAY, FISHING THE RIVER TAY AT PERTH HARBOUR IN SCOTLAND. DAIWA SALES DIRECTOR, JOHN MIDDLETON HAS BROUGHT ME TO THIS BIG ROACH HOTSPOT. I'M GOING TO PUT A PROTOTYPE OF THE NEW DAIWA HARRIER TOURNAMENT ROD THROUGH ITS PACES.

JOHN'S LOOSE FEEDING OVER HIS GROUNDBAIT BUT I'M STARTING A LITTLE MORE CAUTIOUSLY, JUST PUTTING IN REGULAR, SMALLER BALLS OF CASTER-LACED FEED. ALTHOUGH WE'RE 20 MILES FROM THE SEA THERE'S A HUGE RISE AND FALL OF TIDE IN THE HARBOUR AND IT CAN ONLY BE FISHED ON THE EBB. WE'VE HIT IT JUST RIGHT — THE TIDE IS RUNNING OUT UNTIL LATE AFTERNOON.

THAT WAS A BITE! DIDN'T TAKE LONG TO GET A RESPONSE ON DOUBLE MAGGOT. I MISSED THAT ONE BUT I'VE GOT A FEELING THIS IS GOING TO BE A GREAT SESSION. IT'S REALLY MILD FOR MID-WINTER — I'M IN SHIRTSLEEVES.

I DON'T BELIEVE IT. I'VE DROPPED THIS ONE TOO! WHAT ON EARTH'S GOING ON?

THEN JOHN PUTS AN END TO HIS SEQUENCE OF MISSED BITES. HE'S STEPPED UP THE BREAD FEED AND THE ROACH HAVE REALLY GOT THEIR HEADS DOWN.

A NICE 1lb PLUS ROACH.

MY TURN AT LAST AS I FINALLY SUCCEED IN NETTING A GOOD ROACH. THE AVERAGE SIZE OF THE FISH IN THIS HARBOUR LOOKS EXCEPTIONAL.

THE REEL FITTING ON THIS TOP OF THE RANGE *TOURNAMENT* ROD GIVES ABSOLUTE SECURITY. THE REEL SLOTS INTO A RECESS AND THE FRONT PART OF THE HANDLE SCREWS DOWN OVER IT.

FLAT TO SIT SECURELY UNDER ARM.

THERE ARE ALSO TWO 3in EXTENSION PIECES ON THE BUTT WHICH I'VE UNSCREWED AS I PREFER A SHORT HANDLE.

JOHN'S USING THE TOURNAMENT AT ITS FULL LENGTH OF 13ft 4in. HE'S PUT 4 BALLS OF GROUNDBAIT OUT TO START WITH — LOADED WITH CASTERS AND NEAT ESSENCE OF MALT FLAVOURING.

ISLAND

DOCKSIDE

TO DUNDEE AND THE SEA

WE ARE HERE

THE ROACH ARE ATTRACTED OUT OF THE MAIN RIVER INTO THIS DEAD ARM BY GRAIN SHIPS BEING UNLOADED ON THE WHARF. I CAN SEE SOYA MEAL PARTICLES SCATTERED OVER THE SURFACE. THOUSANDS OF SPECIMEN ROACH GATHER HERE FOR A FREE MEAL.

I'VE HIT THIS ONE, FEELS LIKE A GOOD FISH TOO ...

AH! IT'S COME OFF.

THERE'S A LOT OF FISH OUT THERE. THEY'RE MOVING UP IN THE WATER TO INTERCEPT MY GROUNDBAIT ON-THE-DROP — I HOOKED THAT ONE WELL OFF THE BOTTOM.

I THINK I KNOW NOW WHAT I WAS DOING WRONG. THESE FIGHTING FIT ROACH HAVE VERY HARD MOUTHS — THE HOOK FELL OUT AS I WAS LANDING THIS ONE. THE NEW TOURNAMENT ROD IS A LITTLE SOFTER THAN I'M USED TO — I WASN'T SETTING THE HOOK PROPERLY.

YES! A HARDER STRIKE THIS TIME AND THE FISH FEELS WELL AND TRULY HOOKED — THIS ROD IS REALLY NICE. IT'LL HOLD LIGHT LINES EXTREMELY WELL I RECKON. ON A 1-7lb BOTTOM IT JUST NEEDS A FRACTION MORE FORCE ON THE STRIKE.

River Tay Continued

● Roach and pike have always been the traditional targets in lochs and rivers for the small band of Scottish coarse anglers. But clandestine stocking has resulted in a richer mix of species. For instance, there are now shoals of chub and dace in the Clyde and even small pockets of barbel close to Glasgow city centre.

JOHN MIDDLETON IS LOWER DOWN AT WATER LEVEL AND HE IS FINDING THAT MORE CONVENTIONAL TACKLE WORKS FINE. HE'S STEPPED UP THE GROUNDBAIT FEED AND THE BIG ROACH, BETWEEN 1¼-1½lb, ARE COMING THICK AND FAST.

JOHN'S RIG. HE'S FISHING OVERDEPTH WITH DOUBLE MAGGOT HOOKBAIT.

2 SSG

2.5lb

No 6

No 6

1.5lb   No 6

AS YOU BECOME MORE PROFICIENT WITH THE SLIDER, YOU CAN ACTUALLY FISH ON-THE-DROP BY FEATHERING THE LINE OUT. THIS ONLY WORKS WITH LOADED FLOATS. BY SLOWING DOWN THE LINE YOU FEED TO THE FLOAT, IT TAKES SEVERAL SECONDS LONGER TO COCK...

...AND WITH THIS MANY FISH ABOUT IT DOESN'T ALWAYS GET THE CHANCE TO SETTLE AT ALL.

IT'S GETTING HARD TO CONCENTRATE IN THIS AQUARIUM. THERE'S EVEN A 10lb SALMON SWIMMING ABOUT BY MY KEEPNET.

WE'VE BOTH ENJOYED SEVERAL HECTIC HOURS SPORT, BUT SUDDENLY BITES HAVE CEASED. I CAN SEE THE REASON WHY- ON THE FAR SIDE THE WATER LEVEL MARKER SHOWS THE TIDE IS FLOODING BACK FAST.

JOHN'S WEIGHED HIS CATCH AT 30lb AND MANY OF THEM ARE ROACH SCALING 1¼lb OR MORE.

I'VE JUST LANDED MY FIRST TAY ROACH FROM PERTH HARBOUR AFTER MISSING A SERIES OF BOLD BITES. I'M GETTING USED TO THE NEW DAIWA TOURNAMENT ROD...

... BUT I'M NOT HAPPY WITH MY END TACKLE. SITTING THIS HIGH UP AND CASTING A LONG WAY OUT IN 7 Ft OF WATER IS MAKING IT DIFFICULT TO HIT BITES CONSTANTLY. MAYBE THE SOLUTION IS A BOTTOM END SLIDER.

IAN HEAPS SEMI-LOADED BODIED SLIDER

SLIDING STOP KNOT

No 6

3 AAA

No 8

THAT'S MUCH MORE POSITIVE ON THE STRIKE. I'M NO LONGER HAVING TO SET THE HOOK BY STRIKING THROUGH THE FLOAT. A SLIDER DOESN'T IMPEDE THE STRIKE AT ALL.

JOHN IS A VERY PROFICIENT ANGLER. THE ONLY THING THAT STOPS HIM FIGURING MORE PROMINENTLY ON THE MATCH CIRCUIT IS IRONICALLY DAIWA'S SUCCESS STORY. THIS IS ONLY THE SECOND CHANCE HE'S HAD TO BE ON THE BANK FOR SEVERAL MONTHS.

I'M ALSO CATCHING WELL NOW ON THE SLIDER AND HAVE STOPPED BUMPING FISH. THE FLOAT POPS UP FLAT ON THE SURFACE ON THE STRIKE, AS THE LINE RUNS SWEETLY THROUGH THE BOTTOM EYE ATTACHMENT.

Tony Whieldon

I THOUGHT THIS ONE WAS A BIT LIVELY — IT'S A 1 lb SEA TROUT!

MY ROACH NET WENT 27 lb. I HAD MORE FISH, BUT NOT SO MANY 1 lb PLUS SPECIMENS. I ALSO TOOK 4 TROUT AND TWO SMALL SALMON PARR WHICH WENT STRAIGHT BACK.

THE WATER'S NEARLY AT OUR FEET NOW. JOHN ONCE GOT STRANDED ON AN ISLAND IN THE TAY, SO WE'D BETTER BE OFF. WHAT A FANTASTIC DAY'S ROACH SPORT. I DIDN'T REALISE SCOTLAND WAS THIS GOOD. NOW I KNOW WHAT TO DO HERE I FEEL 50 lb IS EASILY ON THE CARDS.

FEBRUARY
Small Estate Lake
Guildford, Surrey

THE WATER APPEARS BADLY SILTED AND COVERS ABOUT 1½ ACRES. ANDY IS CONCENTRATING AROUND A FALLEN TREE. HE'LL TRY STALKING WITH FLOAT TACKLE AT (A) AND FISH SEMI-BOLT RIGS AT (B) AND (C). I'M STARTING ON THE POLE IN THE DEEPER WATER.

INLET

SHALLOWS 12-14 in

ANDY'S PITCH — (A)

— (B)

18 in — 2 ft

(C)

2 ft 6 in   2 ft 6 in

3 ft   3 ft   3 ft

4 ft   4 ft   4 ft

DAM   OUTLET   MY SWIM

ANDY LITTLE HAS JOINED ME TODAY ON THIS ATTRACTIVE, SMALL LAKE — WE'VE BEEN INVITED OVER FOR A TEST FISH TO INVESTIGATE THE POTENTIAL.

I'VE STARTED ON BREADPUNCH, FEEDING TINY PUFFS OF CLOUDY BROWN CRUMB AT 7 METRES...

...AND CATCH A SMALL ROACH FIRST CAST.

MY LIGHT RIG IS FINDING SMALL ROACH AND SKIMMERS EVERY CAST— GREAT IN A MATCH, BUT A BIT BORING WHEN PLEASURE FISHING. I'VE TAKEN 30 FISH ALREADY WITH NO SIGN OF BETTER QUALITY SAMPLES MOVING IN.

A LOVELY SIX POUND COMMON

I'VE JOINED ANDY TO CHAT ABOUT HIS METHODS. HIS MEAT BAIT, CAST TOWARDS THE FAR BANK, HAS BEEN PICKED UP BY A VERY BIG FISH. AH! BAD LUCK— THE HOOK'S PULLED FREE.

ANDY'S SET-UPS

14lb Drennan Double Strength

LUNCHEON MEAT RIG

Anti-tangle tubing

1¼oz weight forced over

Swivel partly jammed in tubing

10lb black Dacron

White dental floss

No.10 Drennan Super Specialist

FLOAT RIG
Baits: worm and meat

Drennan crystal insert waggler

Large DAM sliding rubber float stops

Bulk shot

10lb black Dacron

Super Specialist

MY POLE RIG

Stillwater Ignesti pole float

Stabilising styls

1·1lb main line

Bulk styls

9½oz hooklength

Smaller dropper styls

22 Gamakatsu hook

TIME FOR A CHANGE OF TACTICS — TEN BIG BALLS OF GROUNDBAIT LACED WITH PLENTY OF CASTERS, CHOPPED WORMS AND RED PINKIES ARE PUT OUT AT 9 METRES. HOPEFULLY THIS WILL FEED OFF THE SMALL STUFF AND DRAW IN THE BIGGER FISH.

FIRST LINE

MEANWHILE ANDY HAS HIT INTO A POWERFUL FISH ON HIS FLOAT GEAR.

MY SWIM'S HAD PLENTY OF TIME TO SETTLE AFTER THE BOMBARDMENT, BUT STRAIGHT AWAY I'M GETTING A SMALL FISH A CHUCK AGAIN — TIME TO MOVE AND TRY SOMETHING ELSE.

MEANWHILE, ANDY'S ALSO DECIDED TO MOVE AFTER LOSING THAT BIG FISH. HE'S PUT A BED OF LUNCHEON MEAT DOWN BY THE OVERHANGING BUSHES IN SOME DEEPER WATER IN THE CORNER OF THE DAM...

FLOAT RIG WITH WORM

MEAT

MEAT

...SUDDENLY HIS OPTONIC SIGNALS A SCREAMING RUN.

LINE IS TUMBLING FROM HIS REEL AT A FAST RATE OF KNOTS...

Estate Lake Continued

● Never take anything for granted in coarse fishing. This beautiful, old estate lake might appear to be stuffed with stunted roach and a few middleweight carp but there was at least one pike in the water nearing 20 lb and a posse of 3 lb perch. Fish populations fluctuate for all sorts of reasons and even a water past its peak is capable of springing a surprise.

ANDY LITTLE HAS STRUCK INTO A BIG FISH AFTER A SCREAMING RUN ON HIS ROD POSITIONED NEAREST THE OVERHANGING BUSHES.

AFTER A SHORT STRUGGLE THE LARGE LANDING NET GOES UNDER THE FISH...

MEANWHILE

I'VE MOVED SWIMS AND FIRST CAST, AFTER CHANGING TO THE WAGGLER, I ALSO HIT INTO SOMETHING A BIT BETTER— A 12oz SKIMMER.

I'M FISHING A 2 AAA WAGGLER FIVE ROD LENGTHS OUT AND TAKING FISH STEADILY ON SINGLE WHITE MAGGOT.

ANDY'S SWIM ALSO SEEMS TO HAVE GONE QUIET. ALL HE'S GETTING ARE LINE BITES — ODD, SHORT BLEEPS ON THE OPTONICS.

THE SMALL ROACH ARE BACK IN MY SWIM AGAIN — IT'S A FISH A CHUCK— THEN ANOTHER DEAD SPELL.

CATAPULTING SMALL CLOUDY BALLS OF GROUNDBAIT ONTO THE WAGGLER LINE BRINGS A FEW SMALL BONUS SKIMMERS, BUT BIGGER FISH ARE STILL NOT SHOWING.

THE CARP MAKES A BID FOR THE COVER. ANDY HOLDS IT HARD AND THE FISH SPLASHES ON THE SURFACE, SENDING SHOCK WAVES ACROSS THE LAKE.

...A FIT LOOKING 14½lb MIRROR.

JUST AS I WAS BUILDING THE SWIM NICELY THE BITES CEASED. I NOTICED THIS A COUPLE OF TIMES IN THE PREVIOUS SWIM — COULD BE A PIKE MOVING IN I SUPPOSE.

ABOUT 100 FISH FOR 6lb. DISAPPOINTING REALLY, CONSIDERING THIS WATER IS NOT NORMALLY FISHED. I'VE A FEELING THESE SMALL ROACH AND SKIMMERS ARE STUNTED...

...THEN AGAIN, ANDY'S TWO CARP LOOKED HEALTHY ENOUGH. THINK I'LL HAVE TO GIVE THIS PLACE ANOTHER GO WITH A DIFFERENT BAIT AND METHOD.

THESE OLD ESTATE LAKES ARE TRULY INTRIGUING WATERS.

FEBRUARY
River Great Ouse
Newport Pagnell, Buckinghamshire

COLIN'S FISHING ABOVE ME ON A NARROWER SECTION AND HAS HIT INTO A BIG FISH STRAIGHT AWAY....

.... ONLY FOR THE HOOK TO PULL FREE AT THE NET. IT WAS A GOOD CHUB.

AT LAST COLIN MANAGES TO DRAW THE FISH TO THE LANDING NET AND REALISES IT'S HIS FIRST EVER BARBEL.

HE'S DELIGHTED! A WELL CONDITIONED FISH OF JUST UNDER 5lb.

AT LAST! A POSITIVE BITE, RIGHT DOWN THE SWIM.

THAT'S BETTER. A 2½lb CHUB.

I TOOK HALF-A-DOZEN SMALL ROACH AND DACE AFTER THAT CHUB BEFORE THE SWIM DRIED UP. I'VE CAST A BOMB RIG BACK INTO THE DEEPER WATER TO SEE IF I CAN DISCOVER WHAT THOSE TINY INDICATIONS WERE BEING CAUSED BY. I'VE ANTICIPATED ONE AND IT'S A REASONABLE FISH.

I'M FISHING THE LINEAR FISHERIES STRETCH OF THE UPPER OUSE IN BUCKINGHAMSHIRE WITH LOCAL BAILIFF COLIN COLBECK WHO WAS THE ORIGINAL CAPTAIN OF THE WELL KNOWN BLACK HORSE MATCHFISHING OUTFIT. HE'S RECOMMENDED THIS SWIM — IT CAN TURN UP BIG CHUB, BREAM AND QUALITY ROACH.

EDDY (BREAM)

ROACH

CHUB

SHALLOWS (CHUB)

I'VE STARTED OFF SEARCHING OUT THE SWIM WITH A WAGGLER RIG. THOSE RUSHES LOOK INVITING, BUT THE DEEPER WATER IN THE FAR BANK EDDY SHOULD HOLD THE BREAM. I'LL SPREAD MY LOOSE FED CASTERS ABOUT UNTIL I GET A BITE.

I'VE ONLY TAKEN ONE GUDGEON ON THE FLOAT. THE WEATHER'S GETTING REALLY NASTY — RAIN AND GALE FORCE WIND. LET'S TRY THE BOMB.

COLIN'S GONE A LONG TIME WITHOUT A BITE SO HE'S SCALED DOWN TO A 1lb BOTTOM. THIS BRINGS A BOLD BITE ON A SINGLE MAGGOT HOOKBAIT — BUT IT'S CERTAINLY NO CHUB THIS TIME. THE FISH HAS RUN UPSTREAM AND THREATENS TO DISAPPEAR AROUND THE NEXT BEND.

MEANWHILE

I COULD ONLY ATTRACT TINY INDICATIONS ON THE QUIVERTIP. THE DEEPER WATER WON'T RESPOND TO THE WAGGLER SO I'VE BEEN FLICKING A FEW MAGGOTS DOWNSTREAM INTO THE SHALLOWS. LET'S RUN A FLOAT DOWN THERE.

DAMN! THE HOOK PULLED FREE — FELT LIKE A GOOD ROACH TOO.

A BIT DISAPPOINTING, JUST THE ONE CHUB AND A SMATTERING OF BITS. THE RIVER WAS SOCK-ON A WEEK AGO BUT THE COLOUR'S DROPPED OUT AND THE WIND AND RAIN MADE TACKLE PRESENTATION VERY DIFFICULT. WONDER WHERE THOSE BREAM ARE HIDING?

MARCH
Twyford Farm
Warwickshire Avon

DESPITE HIS OBVIOUS DISAPPOINTMENT AT BEING PIPPED AT THE POST FOR THE MATCHMAN OF THE YEAR TITLE, PAUL NEWELL IS FISHING BRILLIANTLY. HE'S WON 3 MIDWEEK OPENS IN THE SPACE OF SIX DAYS. TODAY HE STARTS THE MATCH ON A STICK FLOAT RIG...

TODAY I'M FISHING A MATCH ON THE WARWICKSHIRE AVON AT TWYFORD WITH NEW SHAKESPEARE MATCHMAN OF THE YEAR DAVE HARRELL AND RUNNER-UP PAUL NEWELL. DAVE'S NOT DRAWN BADLY ON WILMOTS (PEG 2) AND PAUL'S GOT A GOOD 'UN TOO, PEG 10 AT WILMOTS — OPPOSITE THE MOUTH OF A BROOK. I'VE BEEN DRAWING REALLY BADLY LATELY. YES, I'VE DONE IT AGAIN! PEG 105, A REAL NO-HOPER THEY TELL ME.

DAVE HARRELL IS FISHING A SIMILAR TWO-PRONGED APPROACH BUT IS USING A 14 METRE POLE FOR THE NEARSIDE LINE.

MY SWIM IS A RIGHT 'BIRDCAGE' HIGH BANK BEHIND AND SURROUNDED BY TREES AND BUSHES. THE WAGGLER IS OUT, WITH SLACK ACROSS AND THE MAIN FLOW 1/3RD OF THE WAY OUT. I'LL START ON 9 METRES OF POLE, BUT THE INSIDE FLOW IS VERY ERRATIC.

NOTHING ON THE POLE AS YET, SO LET'S TRY THE MAGGOT FEEDER ACROSS. I'M NOT THAT CONFIDENT — THE ONLY FAR-BANK FEATURE IS ANOTHER FISHING STAGE.

IT'S A CLOSE BATTLE WITH DAVE HARRELL WHO'S ALSO CATCHING A FEW ON THE POLE.

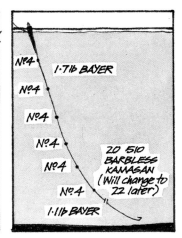

Nº4

1.7lb BAYER

Nº4

Nº4

Nº4

Nº4

20 510
BARBLESS
KAMASAN
(Will change to
22 later)

Nº4

1.1lb BAYER

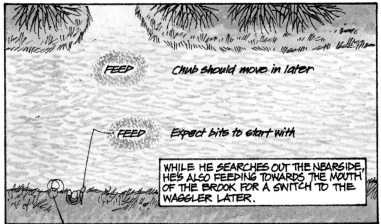

FEED — *Chub should move in later*

FEED — *Expect bits to start with*

WHILE HE SEARCHES OUT THE NEARSIDE, HE'S ALSO FEEDING TOWARDS THE MOUTH OF THE BROOK FOR A SWITCH TO THE WAGGLER LATER.

AGAIN HE HOPES TO FEED UP HIS MAIN FAR SIDE LINE TO GET THE FISH CONFIDENT BEFORE HE GOES OVER ON THE WAGGLER. HE'S CONTENT WITH A FEW SMALL, NEAR-SIDE FISH TO BEGIN WITH.

6 Ft

DAVE EXPECTS CHUB ON HIS WAGGLER RIG IN THE LAST TWO HOURS AS THE LIGHT FADES.

STRAIGHT PEACOCK WAGGLER LOCKED BY 3 AAA + 1 BB

Nº6

1 lb HOOKLENGTH AND 22 HOOK

Nº6

2 lb OMNI MAIN LINE

Nº8

Nº8

MEANWHILE PAUL'S STEADY LOOSE FEEDING WITH BRONZE MAGGOTS IS BRINGING HIM A FEW SMALL FISH TO THE STICK FLOAT.

THE RIVER'S SLIGHTLY COLOURED AND RISING — PERFECT REALLY, AND YET I'M GETTING MINNOWED OUT ON THE FEEDER.

THE FLOW'S TOO ERRATIC ON THE INSIDE FOR THE STICK FLOAT, IT STOPS ALTOGETHER ONE MINUTE AND THEN ROCKETS THROUGH THE NEXT. I MUST ADMIT WITH NEARLY TWO HOURS GONE I'M STUMPED.

Warwickshire Avon Continued

● Matches along the Avon are among the most competitive in the country. On popular stretches like Twyford Farm, matchmen know the precise potential of each and every swim and the best methods to adopt. There is really no need for coarse fish surveys on waters like this – the matchmen soon know if there has been the slightest shift in fish numbers!

MATCHMAN OF THE YEAR DAVE HARRELL HAS TAKEN A FEW BITS ON HIS POLE. NOW HE'S MOVING HIS ATTACK ACROSS THE RIVER, HOPING FOR CHUB ON THE WAGGLER...

MY MATCH ON THE WARWICKSHIRE AVON AT TWYFORD IS GOING BADLY. I'VE ONLY TAKEN A RUFFE AND A GUDGEON FROM AN UNFANCIED PEG. THE FAR SIDE FEEDER LINE IS ALIVE WITH MINNOWS AND THE INSIDE FLOW IS ALL OVER THE PLACE.

ARCH RIVAL PAUL NEWELL IS ALSO ON THE WAGGLER, HE'S LANDING A 1lb CHUB.

WHILE THERE'S ANOTHER DING-DONG BATTLE GOING ON BETWEEN DAVE AND PAUL, I'M STILL SEARCHING FOR A TAKING METHOD. I SPOTTED A BLEAK TOPPING SO I'VE QUICKLY SET UP A SURFACE RIG ON A SIX METRE POLE.

I'LL PUT IN SOME SLOPPY GROUNDBAIT EVERY CAST WITH A FEW FREE PINKIE OFFERINGS.

SLIM POLE FLOAT

10oz

SMALL BULK (No 9s)

22 BARBLESS

THIS IS BETTER. I'VE TAKEN 16 OF THESE HUGE BLEAK IN 16 CHUCKS

WITH JUST AN HOUR TO GO I'VE GOT ABOUT 3lb OF GUDGEON AND BLEAK, NOT ENOUGH I FEEL FOR A SECTION WIN. I NOTICED A BIG FISH ROLL OVER BY THE FAR BANK STAGING — COULD HAVE BEEN A PIKE....

...BUT I'LL TRY A BIGGER HOOK AND SOME LUNCHEON MEAT ON A STRAIGHT BOMB RIG JUST IN CASE IT WAS A CHUB OR BARBEL.

.... DAVE'S WINNING TECHNIQUE INVOLVES VERY REGULAR HELPINGS OF LOOSE FED MAGGOTS.

HE HOOKS A SMALL CHUB — IF HE CAN PUT A FEW OF THESE TOGETHER HE COULD START TO BUILD A WINNING WEIGHT.

PAUL KEEPS THE LOOSE FED BRONZE MAGGOTS GOING IN TOO, HOPING FOR CHUB ON-THE-DROP FROM THE MOUTH OF THE STREAM OPPOSITE.

WELL I DON'T BELIEVE THIS. I WAS JUST SORTING OUT MY GEAR FOR A BIG BLEAK WEIGHT AND THEY'VE GONE AS QUICKLY AS THEY ARRIVED.

PUTTING THAT GROUNDBAIT IN HAS BROUGHT A BONUS — I'M GETTING SOME BIG GUDGEON ON MY ORIGINAL POLE RIG NOW. IT'S A MISERABLE DAY, THE RAIN IS BUCKETING DOWN.

THAT LAST HOUR GAMBLE BACKFIRED I SAT IT OUT ON THE MEAT TO AVOID THE MINNOWS BUT DIDN'T GET THE FISH I SO BADLY NEEDED.

AFTER WEIGHING IN 3lb·3oz I FIND I ONLY NEEDED 3 MORE OUNCES TO WIN THE SECTION! SHOULD HAVE STAYED ON THE GUDGEON!

BACK ON WILMOTS PAUL HAS PIPPED DAVE HARRELL BY 2 OUNCES, BUT IT'S A SPLIT SECTION. PAUL WINS HIS HALF WITH 5·10·8, DAVE WINS HIS WITH 5·8·8. YOU JUST CAN'T KEEP THESE TWO DOWN!

RESULT
1st. S. JACKSON (AVON BAIT) 13·15·0
2nd. P. KILBRIDE (STRATFORD) 11·13·0
3rd. B. CLULEY (DAM STARLETS) 8·0·0

MARCH
River Lea
Cheshunt, Hertfordshire

I'M FISHING 10½ METRES OUT, PRESENTING MY RIG JUST UP THE LEDGE ON THE FAR SIDE. I'VE TRIED PUTTING IN NEAT JOKERS BUT WITHOUT RESPONSE. NOW I'LL TRY SIX BALLS OF JOKER LACED GROUNDBAIT. A BIT EXTREME, BUT THE DISTURBANCE OFTEN BRINGS IN SOME FISH, AND SURPRISINGLY QUICKLY.

MY MATCHFISHING MATES TOLD ME OF SOME FINE ROACH AND BLEAK WEIGHTS ON THE LEA NAVIGATION AT CHESHUNT AND I'VE DECIDED TO INVESTIGATE WITH THE LONG POLE AND BLOODWORM. TO MY RIGHT IS BRITISH GROUNDBAITS ANGLER STEVE LINNEY — HE'S GOING FOR THE BLEAK.

I COULDN'T GET A BITE IN THE FIRST SWIM SO I'VE MOVED UP NEAR THE LOCK. STEVE'S STRUGGLING TOO AND HAS ALSO SWITCHED SWIMS TO FISH OPPOSITE A BOAT TURNING BAY. HE RECKONS THE WATER'S A LOT CLEARER THAN WHEN IT PRODUCED THE GOOD WEIGHTS IN A MATCH THREE DAYS AGO.

AH, A BITE AT LAST!

A TINY PERCH.

SUDDENLY TINY FISH SCATTER ACROSS THE SURFACE ON THE FAR BANK. MAYBE PIKE ARE PUTTING MY SWIM DOWN.

I QUICKLY SET UP A MAKESHIFT PIKE RIG, LIP HOOKING A SMALL BLEAK. I HAVEN'T GOT ANY TRACE WIRE WITH ME AND USE A LENGTH OF 15lb DACRON INSTEAD. THIS IS NOT RECOMMENDED FOR SERIOUS PIKING BUT I'M ONLY EXPECTING JACKS.

ALL BALSA CHUBBER FLOAT

AAA SSG

4lb

15lb DACRON

No 6 HOOK

I CAST THE RIG OVER TOWARDS THE FAR BANK SHELF AND THE FLOAT SHOOTS AWAY IMMEDIATELY!

POLE CUP CLIPPED ON TO POLE

TURNED OVER TO RELEASE JOKERS ACCURATELY

CANAL VENUES WILL USUALLY ONLY TAKE ONE BOMBARDMENT, THEN IT'S A CASE OF TOPPING UP THE SWIM OCCASIONALLY WITH NEAT BAIT. A POLE CUP IS VERY ACCURATE, OR JOKERS. CAN BE FED IN LEAM WHICH BINDS THEM IN A BALL AND ADDS ENOUGH WEIGHT TO PROPEL SMALL HELPINGS A LONG WAY.

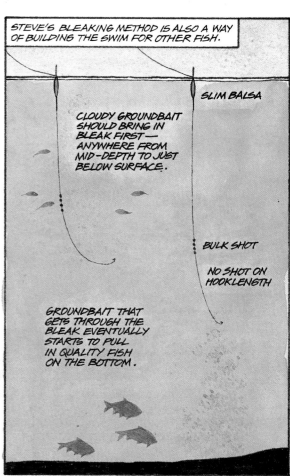

STEVE'S BLEAKING METHOD IS ALSO A WAY OF BUILDING THE SWIM FOR OTHER FISH.

SLIM BALSA

CLOUDY GROUNDBAIT SHOULD BRING IN BLEAK FIRST — ANYWHERE FROM MID-DEPTH TO JUST BELOW SURFACE.

BULK SHOT

NO SHOT ON HOOKLENGTH

GROUNDBAIT THAT GETS THROUGH THE BLEAK EVENTUALLY STARTS TO PULL IN QUALITY FISH ON THE BOTTOM.

I'VE CAUGHT HALF-A-DOZEN BLEAK IN QUICK SUCCESSION. NO SIGN OF ANYTHING ELSE THOUGH.

NOTHING FOR AN HOUR AFTER THAT PERCH. I'VE NOTICED THERE'S A FAIR FLOW COMING THROUGH THE LOCK GATES, LET'S TRY HERE.

A NICE 5lb PIKE IT GAVE A GOOD SCRAP ON MY MATCH ROD!

STEVE'S ONLY BITE OF THE DAY CAME FROM A 14oz SKIMMER. AFTER THAT PIKE. I HAD ONE OTHER RUN WHICH I MISSED THEN I COULDN'T CATCH ANOTHER BLEAK FOR BAIT. THERE WERE PIKE EVERYWHERE. THINK I'LL TRY HERE AGAIN, ONLY NEXT TIME I'LL COME BETTER PREPARED.

River Lea Continued

● Like the majority of our rivers, the Lea is unrecognisable from the meandering, overgrown waterway of Izaak Walton's day. Bends and bankside cover have been obliterated. Heavy industry and ugly housing estates crowd its banks. But somehow the resilient coarse fish stocks survive the pressures of the 20th century and provide a means of escapism for millions . . .

THERE SEEMS TO BE A HUGE SHOAL TUCKED RIGHT IN THE MOUTH OF THE LOCK. I'M GETTING THEM QUITE FAST.

I'VE BROUGHT DEADBAITS AND SPINNERS WITH ME TODAY TO HAVE A GO FOR THE PIKE WHICH WERE VERY ACTIVE LAST WEEK. LET'S JUST SEE IF THE BLEAK ARE STILL AROUND FIRST.

SLIM BALSA BLEAKER
4ft
BULK No 10s
9oz
22 BARBLESS

Tony Whieldon

NOTHING. THE IRONY IS THAT THE WATER'S A LOT MORE COLOURED THIS WEEK AND I HAVEN'T GOT BLOODWORM AND JOKER WITH ME. I BET IF I HAD I'D HAVE A NETFULL OF ROACH.

LET'S TRY A DEADBAIT ON THE FAR SHELF.

DEADBAIT RIG
SSG   SSG
SINGLE HOOK WIRE TRACE
LIP HOOKED DEADBAIT

I'M USING A STYL RIG AND PICKING THE FISH UP BY TRIPPING A SINGLE PINKIE ALONG THE BOTTOM.

THIN BALSA FLOAT WITH WIRE STEM

BULK STYLS

SMALL STYL DROPPERS

THAT'S AMAZING – A BITE STRAIGHT AWAY FROM A 4oz ROACH . . . .

. . . . AND ANOTHER.

PIKE ACTIVITY AREA LAST WEEK.

THESE FRENCH BLEAK FLOATS REALLY ARE VERY GOOD. THEY'RE PAINTED A LIGHT GREY SO YOU CAN SPOT THEM TILTING OVER IF A BLEAK RUNS WITH THE BAIT.

BLEAK

WELL, THE BLEAK MUST BE SHOALED UP TIGHT IN THE LOCK MOUTH FOR A REASON. LET'S TRY THE SURROUNDING WATER WITH A PLUG.

THE DEADBAIT DOESN'T SEEM TO BE PULLING ANY ATTENTION. I THINK I'LL TRY THE LONG POLE. I'LL PUT HALF-A-DOZEN BALLS OF PINKIE LACED GROUNDBAIT IN AT 10 METRES.

THE FISH ARE A LOT MORE ACTIVE THAN LAST WEEK. BY FEEDING CLOUDY GROUNDBAIT AND A FEW PINKIES I'M GETTING PLENTY OF BITES.

HOW IRONIC, LAST WEEK I HAD THE BAIT TO DO THIS AND GOT PESTERED BY PIKE, TODAY I ONLY HAD HALF A PINT OF PINKIES AND I'VE CAUGHT LOADS OF ROACH AND PERCH.

APRIL
River Shannon
Eire

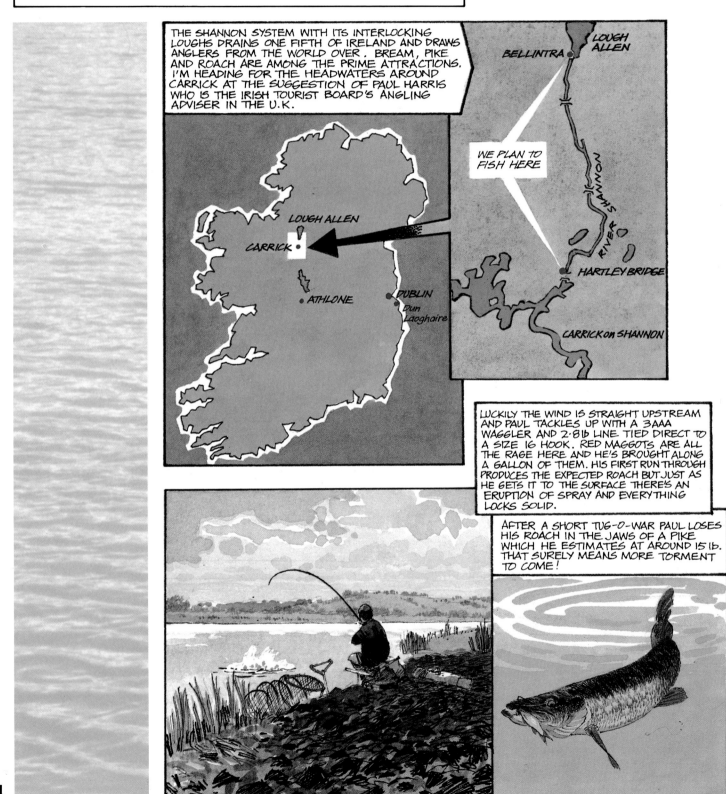

THE SHANNON SYSTEM WITH ITS INTERLOCKING LOUGHS DRAINS ONE FIFTH OF IRELAND AND DRAWS ANGLERS FROM THE WORLD OVER. BREAM, PIKE AND ROACH ARE AMONG THE PRIME ATTRACTIONS. I'M HEADING FOR THE HEADWATERS AROUND CARRICK AT THE SUGGESTION OF PAUL HARRIS WHO IS THE IRISH TOURIST BOARD'S ANGLING ADVISER IN THE U.K.

WE PLAN TO FISH HERE

BELLINTRA
LOUGH ALLEN
RIVER SHANNON
HARTLEY BRIDGE
CARRICK on SHANNON

LOUGH ALLEN
CARRICK
ATHLONE
DUBLIN
Dun Laoghaire

LUCKILY THE WIND IS STRAIGHT UPSTREAM AND PAUL TACKLES UP WITH A 3AAA WAGGLER AND 2·8lb LINE TIED DIRECT TO A SIZE 16 HOOK. RED MAGGOTS ARE ALL THE RAGE HERE AND HE'S BROUGHT ALONG A GALLON OF THEM. HIS FIRST RUN THROUGH PRODUCES THE EXPECTED ROACH BUT JUST AS HE GETS IT TO THE SURFACE THERE'S AN ERUPTION OF SPRAY AND EVERYTHING LOCKS SOLID.

AFTER A SHORT TUG-O-WAR PAUL LOSES HIS ROACH IN THE JAWS OF A PIKE WHICH HE ESTIMATES AT AROUND 15 lb. THAT SURELY MEANS MORE TORMENT TO COME!

THE SEALINK FERRY CROSSING FROM HOLYHEAD IN NORTH WALES TO DUN LAOGHAIRE TAKES PRECISELY 3½ HOURS. THIS IS MY FIRST TRIP TO IRELAND AND I'M IMPRESSED WITH THE EASE AND SPEED OF THE OPERATION. VIRTUALLY EVERY OTHER CAR IS SPROUTING ROD-HOLDALLS. MOST OF THE GROUPS ARE ANGLERS WHO HAVE BEEN FANS OF IRISH FISHING FOR YEARS.

SEAN'S PLAICE IN CARRICK IS A FAVOURITE GUESTHOUSE WITH VISITING ENGLISH ANGLERS AND THAT'S WHERE I MEET UP WITH PAUL HARRIS. HE TELLS ME THE SHANNON BREAM AND ROACH HAVE SHOALED UP LATER THAN USUAL FOR THEIR MASS MIGRATION TO THE SPAWNING GROUNDS. HE'S HEARD OF 70lb BREAM WEIGHTS AT BELLINTRA JUST BELOW LOUGH ALLEN BUT TOMORROW HE WANTS TO TRY NEARBY HARTLEY BRIDGE FOR ROACH.

THE FOLLOWING MORNING IS BRIGHT BUT WINDY WITH A HINT OF RAIN. WE LEAN OVER THE HARTLEY BRIDGE, TRYING TO IMAGINE HOW MANY LAYERS OF ROACH ARE STACKED UP DOWN BELOW. I'M EXPECTING DAVE COSTER TO JOIN US BEFORE LONG. HE'S BEEN FISHING A FESTIVAL IN NORTHERN IRELAND.

RIVER SHANNON
Abhainn na Sionainne
HARTLEY BRIDGE
Roach, Bream, Hybrids Perch Pike
MATCH STRETCH

THIS IS GOING TO BE LIKE A MUDBATH! THE SHANNON HAS ONLY DROPPED WITHIN ITS BANKS IN THE LAST FEW DAYS AND THE MIRE IS KNEE-DEEP IN THE MEADOW. APART FROM THE HOTSPOT ALONGSIDE THE BRIDGE ALL THE SWIMS DOWNSTREAM LOOK AS THOUGH THEY'VE NEVER SEEN A COARSE ANGLER. THAT'S THE BEAUTY OF IRISH FISHING — THERE ARE UNFISHED WATERS AS FAR AS THE EYE CAN SEE.

THEN HE SETTLES INTO A FREE-CATCHING ROUTINE AND STEADILY FEEDS ROACH — ABOUT THREE TO THE POUND — INTO HIS NET.

BUT THE PIKE HAVE OTHER IDEAS. PAUL IS BEING PLAGUED WITH THEM AGAIN AND HAS TO REEL IN HIS ROACH AT HIGH SPEED OTHERWISE THEY GET CHOMPED. FINALLY, HE RIGS UP A PIKE ROD WITH A DEAD ROACH AND FLINGS THE BAIT INTO MIDSTREAM TO TRY A SINK-AND-DRAW RETRIEVE.

THE DEADBAIT IS GRABBED INSTANTLY AND PAUL BACKWINDS ON A POWERFUL FISH. SHANNON PIKE HAVE A FAST TURN OF SPEED AND HE FOLLOWS IT ALONG THE BANK DURING SEVERAL MINUTES OF FURIOUS ACTION UNTIL IT IS READY TO LAND.

'HOW'S IT GOING, LADS?' DAVE COSTER'S GRINNING FACE SUDDENLY APPEARS ON THE BRIDGE ABOVE US AT EXACTLY NOON. AT LEAST SOMETHING'S GOING TO PLAN! MAYBE DAVE CAN FIND A WAY THROUGH THE PIKE.

River Shannon Continued
● Dave Coster joins Westwood at Hartley Bridge to take up the story

THE FLOW HERE IS A LITTLE PACEY AND I'VE PUT MORE SHOT DOWN THE RIG THAN USUAL FOR THIS TYPE OF WAGGLER SET-UP. THE WATER'S VERY CLEAR SO I'M GOING TO FISH A 1lb HOOKLENGTH — LIGHT FOR IRELAND, BUT I'M MAINLY EXPECTING ROACH.

I'VE REALLY BEEN LOOKING FORWARD TO THIS OUTING ON THE SHANNON. LAST TIME I FISHED THE RIVER TWO YEARS AGO I MISSED OUT ON BREAKING THE 100 lb BARRIER ON A MATCH BY JUST ONE FISH. I HAVEN'T GOT LONG TODAY SO ROY WESTWOOD HAS PACKED UP AND PAUL HARRIS IS GOING TO SLOW DOWN ON HIS FEEDING TO GIVE ME A CHANCE TO GET AMONG THE ROACH WHICH ARE SHOALING DOWNSTREAM OF HARTLEY BRIDGE.

DIDN'T TAKE LONG FOR A BITE. NOT A BIG FISH THIS, BUT THE SIGNS ARE THERE THAT THE SWIM'S COMING TO LIFE.

THE WEATHER'S VERY CHANGEABLE THIS AFTERNOON — I HAVE TO KEEP SWITCHING FLOAT TIPS FROM BLACK TO ORANGE SO I CAN SEE WHAT'S GOING ON

I CAN SEE BLACK BETTER WHEN THE SUN'S OUT...

AND HAVE TO CHANGE TO ORANGE WHEN IT'S OVERCAST.

WE'VE ALREADY HAD RAIN SQUALLS — NOW IT'S PELTING DOWN HAIL THE SIZE OF MARBLES.

A PRIME 14 OZ. ROACH.

FOR A MINUTE I THOUGHT I'D CONNECTED WITH A BIG BREAM, BUT IT'S SUDDENLY STEAMED OFF DOWNSTREAM — I RECKON A BIG PIKE'S GRABBED A ROACH.

NEARLY GOT THE PIKE INTO MY NET THERE! HE JUST LET GO OF THE POOR ROACH AT THE LAST MINUTE.

FLOW

SEMI LOADED
(APPROX. 3AAA)
WAGGLER

18 RED
KAMASAN

Nº1
UBLE CUT

2lb

Nº10

1 lb

Nº10

5 Nº8s

I'LL START FEEDING SLOPPY GROUNDBAIT LACED WITH A FEW CASTERS, JUST IN CASE THERE ARE A FEW BREAM ABOUT. ON TOP OF THAT I'LL LOOSE FEED RED MAGGOTS.

MY FIRST FISH WAS A 2oz ROACH. IT'LL BE INTERESTING TO SEE IF I CAN AVOID THE PIKE PROBLEMS ROY AND PAUL WERE EXPERIENCING EARLIER. I'M FISHING A BIT FURTHER ACROSS THAN THEY WERE, BECAUSE I SUSPECT THE PIKE ARE LURKING AROUND A PRONOUNCED LEDGE 10 YARDS OUT.

THE STORM'S OVER AS QUICKLY AS IT BEGAN— BACK TO A BLACK TIP ON THE FLOAT AND I'M INTO A BETTER FISH STRAIGHT AWAY.

IT'S HARD TO KNOW WHAT TO DO HERE, I'M GETTING SHORT SPELLS OF BITES THEN NOTHING. COULD BE THE PIKE CHASING THE ROACH OFF, OR PERHAPS MY GROUNDBAITING IS WRONG. PAUL'S NOT CATCHING ANYTHING NOW.

MAYBE THE GROUNDBAIT IS PULLING TOO MANY SMALL FISH IN AND THEN THE PIKE. I'LL JUST CONCENTRATE ON LOOSE FEED FOR A WHILE AND SEE WHAT HAPPENS.

River Shannon Continued

● The exodus of English anglers to Eire every Close Season is a ritual sustained by unrivalled catches of bream, roach and tench. Thousands cross the sea to fill their nets and recharge their batteries of enthusiasm. Ireland offers stacks more fish than back home and has realised many a dream.

I'VE BEEN EXPERIENCING A BIT OF PIKE TROUBLE AT HARTLEY BRIDGE ON THE SHANNON. I'VE STOPPED USING GROUNDBAIT AND GONE FURTHER OUT ON THE WAGGLER. WHEN I CATCH A ROACH I'M BULLYING IT IN OVER THE NEARSIDE LEDGE — WHERE I SUSPECT THE PIKE ARE LYING UP.

BY JUST LOOSE FEEDING I'VE PULLED THE ROACH UP IN THE WATER. I'VE HAD TO MOVE MY BULK SHOT UP TO COMPENSATE AND THE BITES ARE COMING THICK AND FAST NOW.

PAUL HARRIS OF THE TOURIST BOARD RECKONED THE ROACH WERE RUNNING ON THE QUALITY SIDE HERE YESTERDAY, BUT TODAY THERE ARE LOTS OF SMALL FISH, WHICH IS SLOWING ME DOWN A BIT.

IF THEY WERE ALL THIS SIZE I'D BE ON THE WAY TO A MASSIVE WEIGHT — AS IT IS THOUGH I STILL THINK I'M GOING TO PUT A PRETTY BIG CATCH ON THE SCALES.

HERE WE GO AGAIN! I WAS A FRACTION SLOW WITH THIS ROACH AND A BIG PIKE'S GRABBED IT!

I PLAYED THE PIKE FOR FIVE MINUTES AND HE LET GO LIKE THE LAST ONE SO I'VE GOT MY ROACH BACK.

I'VE MOVED UPSTREAM INTO THE WHITE WATER SWIMS JUST BELOW LOUGH ALLEN. I'VE HEARD BREAM HAVE BEEN MOVING HERE. THE FLOW'S VERY POWERFUL SO IT'S A ROD-IN-THE-AIR JOB TO KEEP THE FEEDER STILL.

A GOOD DROPBACK BITE AND I'M INTO A FISH! THIS FEELS LIKE A BREAM HAS TAKEN MY WORM AND MAGGOT COCKTAIL.

THE FISH FOUGHT WELL IN THE FAST CURRENT AND FELT MUCH BIGGER THAN IT IS — A 1lb SKIMMER.

WHILE THE ROACH ARE UP IN THE WATER I KEEP TRYING THE RIG A LITTLE DEEPER JUST IN CASE ANY BIG BREAM HAVE MOVED IN, BUT THERE'S LOTS OF WEED ON THE BOTTOM AND IT'S DIFFICULT TO GO OVERDEPTH WITHOUT CONSTANTLY DRAGGING UNDER.

BETTER I THINK TO KEEP TAKING FISH UP IN THE WATER. EVERY NOW AND THEN I GET A RUN OF MUCH BETTER SIZED FISH, THIS COMPENSATES FOR THE ODD FLURRIES OF 2oz ROACH.

TIME TO HAVE A LOOK AT SOME BREAM SWIMS FURTHER UPSTREAM. LET'S SEE WHAT I'VE TAKEN...

THERE'S MORE HERE THAN I THOUGHT, ABOUT 25 lb — A NICE NET OF ROACH!

I TOOK FIVE SKIMMERS IN QUICK SUCCESSION AND A SMATTERING OF PERCH, THEN NOTHING. SEEMS THE BIGGER BREAM AREN'T SHOALED HERE TODAY.

TIME FOR A PINT AT SEAN'S PLAICE BACK IN CARRICK. ONE THING THAT'S NOT LACKING IN IRELAND IS HOSPITALITY.

APRIL
Tri-Lakes Fishery
Yateley, Surrey

WIND

FISH BOMB HERE AT 60 YD RANGE WHERE THERE ARE SIGNS OF FISH TOPPING.

I'M FISHING THE LARGER WATER AT THE TRI-LAKES DAY TICKET FISHERY TODAY. THIS POINT SWIM IS A FAVOURITE WITH REGULARS. I'M GOING TO SWITCH BETWEEN THE WAGGLER AND THE BOMB TO TRY AND FIND THE FISH.

I'M PUTTING IN 6 LARGE BALLS OF GROUNDBAIT, LACED WITH CASTER AND MAGGOT, IN THAT CHANNEL BETWEEN THE ISLANDS. I'LL LEAVE THAT LOT TO SETTLE WHILE STARTING ON THE FLOAT.

SHELF

WAGGLER SWIM AT 4 ROD LENGTH

3FT   4FT   5FT

...IT'S A 1½LB TENCH

NEXT CAST RESULTS IN A SKIMMER — THEN EVERYTHING GOES QUIET.

BACK TO THE FLOAT, AND I'VE HOOKED A LIVELY FISH STRAIGHT AWAY...

I'VE A SNEAKING SUSPICION A LOT OF THE BITES ARE BEING CAUSED BY FISH BRUSHING AGAINST MY LINE HIGH IN THE WATER. I'VE SHALLOWED UP TO FISH TWO FEET OFF THE BOTTOM.

THOUGHT SO! A GOOD TENCH RIGHT AWAY— TESTING MY LIGHT TACKLE TO THE LIMIT.

ON THE WAGGLER LINE, I'M LOOSE FEEDING MAGGOTS AND SMALL HELPINGS OF CLOUDY GROUNDBAIT BY CATAPULT.

THERE'S LITTLE WEED GROWTH IN THE OPEN WATER ON THE FLOAT LINE, AND I'VE FOUND A SLIGHT LEDGE ABOUT FOUR ROD LENGTHS OUT. THIS FEATURE SHOULD DRAW FISH EVENTUALLY. I FIND VERY REGULAR, SMALL HELPINGS OF GROUNDBAIT AND LOOSE FEED WORK BEST IN THIS TYPE OF SWIM. CONSTANT FEEDING MAKES UP FOR LACK OF COVER.

SSG AAA
2lb
SMALL SWIVEL
1.1lb
Nº10

AFTER FLOGGING AWAY WITH THE FLOAT FOR TWO HOURS, I'VE BUMPED ONE FISH AND MISSED A COUPLE OF CAGEY BITES. NOW I'VE GONE ONTO THE BOMB, OVER TO MY LEFT, LEAVING THE FIRST SWIM TO SETTLE.

FIRST CAST AND SOMETHING'S SHOWING INTEREST IN MY DOUBLE MAGGOT HOOKBAIT.

THE QUIVERTIP SUDDENLY PULLED ROUND AND I'VE HOOKED INTO A FAIR FISH...

...TURNS OUT TO BE A 3/4 lb CRUCIAN CARP.

I'M GETTING LOADS OF BITES NOW. THE FLOAT'S EITHER SINKING SLOWLY AWAY, SHOOTING UNDER LIKE A BULLET OR LIFTING — TROUBLE IS I'M MISSING THEM.

A NICE 3 POUNDER.

THE SWIM IS REALLY FIZZING WITH BUBBLES — IT'S A BITE A CHUCK — THINGS ARE GETTING INTERESTING!

BY THE LOOKS OF IT THERE'S SOME HUNGRY TENCH OUT THERE...

Tri-Lakes Fishery Continued

● The chain of mature gravel pits to the west of London produce more giant fish than many anglers realise. Numerous 40lb carp have gone unreported because of strict rules of secrecy imposed by the controlling clubs. There are almost certainly British record tench and bream on the loose within 45 minutes of Hyde Park Corner.

REGULAR LOOSE FEEDING IS BRINGING THE FISH UP, BUT AFTER THAT GOOD SPELL THE BITES ARE GETTING HARD TO CONNECT WITH AGAIN.

I'VE STARTED TO CATCH TENCH WELL OFF THE BOTTOM ON MY WAGGLER RIG. THE FISH ARE REALLY FEEDING WELL NOW — A 2½lb TENCH FOLLOWED BY A 1lb CRUCIAN, THEN A 1½ TENCH AND ANOTHER CRUCIAN.

I WONDERED WHAT ON EARTH THAT WAS AT FIRST! ONE OF THE CARP ANGLERS IS USING A RADIO CONTROLLED, MODEL BOAT TO DROP BOILIES BY A BUSH ON THAT ISLAND. THAT'S THE MOST ACCURATE LOOSE FEEDING I'VE EVER SEEN.

I'VE TRIED SWITCHING TO A FEEDER, BUT THE FISH WOULDN'T HAVE IT IN THE SHALLOW WATER. THE BOMB SEEMS BEST — TOPPING THE SWIM UP WITH A COUPLE OF BALLS OF GROUNDBAIT OCCASIONALLY...

...THAT WAS A FINICKY BITE BUT I HIT IT!

NEXT CAST

ANOTHER FISH — THIS ONE TOOK ON THE DROP.

HALF-A-DOZEN HEAVY BALLS OF GROUNDBAIT AND LESS FREQUENT LOOSE FEED PUTS THE FISH DOWN....

... AND IT'S BACK INTO A CATCHING RYTHM AGAIN.

TIME FOR A BREAK AND A CUP OF COFFEE. THE FISH SEEM TO HAVE GONE OFF NOW. I'VE HAMMERED THEM A BIT SO IT'S NOT REALLY SURPRISING.

THE LAKE BEHIND ME IS PACKED WITH SMALL ISLANDS AND TREES. THIS IS WHERE THE CARP ANGLERS REGULARLY HOOK BIG FISH AND THERE'S SEVERAL OF THEM FISHING THE JUNGLE SWIMS TODAY.

AFTER RESTING THE FLOAT SWIM FOR A SHORT WHILE, THE FLOAT RIG FAILS TO BRING ANOTHER RESPONSE.

I'LL FISH OUT THE REST OF THE SESSION ON THE BOMB RIG. I RECKON THIS METHOD IS MORE LIKELY TO FIND A BETTER SIZED FISH.

THE FISH ARE THERE RIGHT AWAY. THEY'VE HAD PLENTY OF TIME TO SETTLE ON THE FEED, WHICH WAS REFLECTED IN THAT CONFIDENT BITE.

THAT WAS A THOROUGHLY INTERESTING DAY'S FISHING — I'VE HAD A GOOD 30lb, MADE UP OF 15 TENCH TO 3lb, 5 CRUCIANS TO 1 lb, AN 8oz SKIMMER AND A 6oz ROACH. THE BOMB RIG ACCOUNTED FOR 10lb OF FISH IN THE LAST HOUR.

43

MAY
Angler's Paradise
Halwill, Devon

I'VE GOT ABOUT 12ft OF WATER ON THE 12m POLE LINE—ONLY TROUBLE IS THE WATER'S PAINFULLY CLEAR.

I'M DOWN IN DEVON AGAIN FOR ANOTHER DIARY SESSION. THIS TIME AT SHOBROOKE LAKE, NEAR CREDITON. I'M FISHING WITH DIARY ARTIST TONY WHIELDON AND EDITOR ROY WESTWOOD. THE EXPECTED SPECIES IN THIS PICTURESQUE LAKE ARE ROACH, PERCH, TENCH AND CARP.

I'M FASCINATED BY THE TENCH LAKE WHICH IS ACTUALLY TENCH SHAPED! I'M GOING TO FISH OUT TO THE CENTRAL ISLAND FROM THIS POINT, WHILE TONY AND ROY FISH THE SMALLER ISLAND AREA.

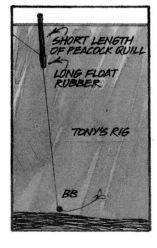

SHORT LENGTH OF PEACOCK QUILL

LONG FLOAT RUBBER

TONY'S RIG

BB

PORCUPINE QUILL

ROY'S RIG

BB

BB

Nº 10

IT'S TAKEN QUITE A TIME TO GET A BITE, TONY AND ROY HAVE BOTH TAKEN SMALL FISH, NOW I'VE GOT ONE!

A SMALL BLUE ORFE, MY FIRST, AND PRETTY LITTLE FISH THEY ARE TOO.

IN THREE HOURS FISHING THIS IS THE ONLY ACTION I'VE HAD. I MOVED INTO SHALLOWER WATER AND PUT A WAGGLER OUT AND AFTER A COUPLE OF FINICKY TOUCHES HOOKED AN EEL OF ABOUT A POUND.

LET'S PUT IT BACK. THE OTHERS HAVEN'T CAUGHT, SO WE'RE GOING TO MAKE A QUICK DASH OVER TO ANGLERS' PARADISE AT BEAWORTHY.

ZYG GREGOREK HAS BUILT SEVERAL INTERESTING LAKES HERE. HE'S MADE ANGLERS PARADISE INTO A SUCCESSFUL VENTURE WHERE ANGLERS CAN ENJOY FIRST CLASS ACCOMMODATION AND INTERESTING, VARIED FISHING.

THE LAKE COMPLEX

BEGINNERS CARP LAKE

TENCH LAKE

E.T. LAKE

MAIN CARP LAKE

PIXIE LAKE

FLOAT FISHING LAKE

FISH FARM

SPECIMEN LAKE

KOI LAKE

THERE'S 3Ft OF WATER JUST OFF THE ISLAND SO I'VE BAITED UP WITH GROUND-BAIT AND HEMP — I'M LOOSE FEEDING MAGGOTS OVER THE TOP.

GROUNDBAIT

LONG INSERT WAGGLER

AAA

BB

Nº 10

Nº 10

THE SPECIES IN HERE ARE BLUE ORFE AND GOLDEN TENCH. I'M USING A LONG INSERT WAGGLER AND HAVE SET THE TACKLE SLIGHTLY OVERDEPTH SO THE LAST Nº 10 RESTS ON THE BOTTOM. THIS DELICATE SET-UP WILL SHOW LIFT BITES AS WELL AS CONVENTIONAL ONES.

I'VE TAKEN HALF A DOZEN SMALL ORFE — NOW I'VE GOT A REALLY POWERFUL FISH ON.

WHAT A BEAUTY! A BLUE ORFE OF A POUND OR SO — THINGS ARE GETTING INTERESTING!

45

Anglers' Paradise Continued

● Zyg Gregorek could not speak a word of English when he arrived here as a Polish refugee. From that unlikely beginning he has built up a booming angling holiday centre in the wilds of Devon with top quality fish stocks bred and reared in his own stewponds.

SURE ENOUGH, THE FLOAT'S SAILED AWAY — THIS IS A GOOD FISH!

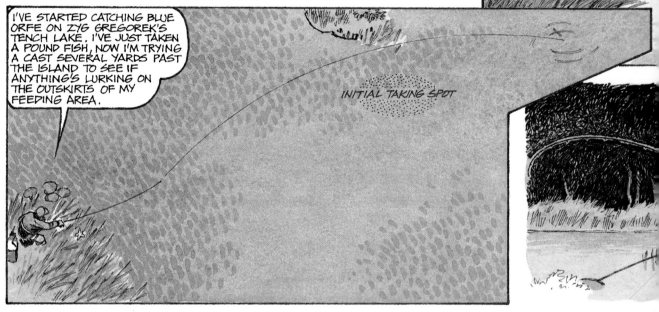

I'VE STARTED CATCHING BLUE ORFE ON ZYG GREGOREK'S TENCH LAKE. I'VE JUST TAKEN A POUND FISH, NOW I'M TRYING A CAST SEVERAL YARDS PAST THE ISLAND TO SEE IF ANYTHING'S LURKING ON THE OUTSKIRTS OF MY FEEDING AREA.

INITIAL TAKING SPOT

MY SWIM HAS DIED A DEATH AFTER THAT FLURRY OF ACTION WITH THE ORFE. I'VE BEEN FEEDING GROUNDBAIT AND LOOSE FEED, BUT I'M NOT CONVINCED THE WATER IS AS COLOURED AS IT LOOKS. THINK I'LL LEAVE THE FORMER ALONE ....

... AND STEP UP THE LOOSE FEED.

THAT CHANGE OF TACTICS HAS BROUGHT BACK THE BITES — SOME ON-THE-DROP.

THIS IS THE FISH I'VE BEEN LOOKING FOR — A LIVELY 1 lb GOLDEN TENCH.

THAT WAS A BIT TOUCH AND GO AT TIMES — THIS THREE POUNDER TESTED MY TACKLE TO THE LIMIT!

WHAT A SMASHING FISH! TO KEEP GOLDEN TENCH LOOKING LIKE THIS ZYG CAN'T AFFORD TO STOCK NORMAL COLOURED FISH BECAUSE THEY WOULD INTERBREED AND LOSE THIS FANTASTIC HUE.

I'VE TAKEN 9 ORFE AND 14 GOLDEN TENCH WHICH PUTS ME WELL INTO DOUBLE FIGURES.

N EVEN BIGGER BLUE
RFE! ZYG HAS DISCOVERED
REALLY HARD FIGHTING
PECIES HERE, I WONDER
HY THESE LOVELY FISH
RE NOT MORE WIDESPREAD?

ROY BEGINS TO HIT
INTO GOLDEN TENCH,
TAKING THE FISH
BY A SMALL ISLAND.

TONY IS ALSO
ENJOYING ACTION
WITH THE TENCH.

NOW I'VE HOOKED A
MUCH BETTER FISH—
THIS ONE'S TRYING TO
GET INTO THE RUSHES
BY THE ISLAND.

WE'VE ALL HAD PLENTY OF FISH. IT'S A
PITY THERE ISN'T ENOUGH TIME TO TRY
SOME OF THE OTHER LAKES, ESPECIALLY
THE LARGER CARP LAKE WHICH HOLDS A
GOOD HEAD OF TWENTIES. THEN AGAIN
THERE'S THE SPECIMEN LAKE WHICH
HOLDS RECORD GOLDEN ORFE ....
I'LL JUST HAVE TO COME BACK HERE!

MAY
Broadland's Fishery
Hampshire

I'M STARTING ON A BIG BODIED WAGGLER, LOCKED BY NEARLY 4 SSGs.

EDITOR, ROY WESTWOOD AND I HAVE BEEN INVITED TO FISH BROADLANDS LAKE, ALONGSIDE THE M27 MOTORWAY IN HAMPSHIRE. FISHERY MANAGER MARK SIMMONDS HAS STOCKED HEAVILY WITH BIG FISH OVER THE PAST DECADE AND WE COULD CATCH ANYTHING FROM OUR SWIM BEHIND THE ISLAND — MAYBE EVEN A RECORD CRUCIAN.

MEANWHILE

ROY'S CATAPULTED KING PRAWN BOILIES UNDERNEATH AN OVERHANGING BRANCH AND ALSO UP AGAINST THE EXPOSED ROOTS OF A TREE WHICH HAS FALLEN ON THE ISLAND, LEAVING A DEPRESSION IN THE MARGINS. THERE'S AN AIR OF EXCITEMENT TODAY BECAUSE A 35lb MIRROR CARP WENT INTO THE WATER RECENTLY.

AS FOR ME, I'LL BE HAPPY TO CONNECT WITH THE PROLIFIC BREAM AND ROACH SHOALS — THIS FEELS LIKE A SKIMMER ALREADY!

MY STEADY FEEDING IS BRINGING PLENTY OF BITES NOW, FIRST FROM SKIMMERS AND QUALITY ROACH . . . .

BY NOW I'M WELL INTO DOUBLE FIGURES ON THE FLOAT, BUT THE WIND PICKS UP AND THIS METHOD DIES.

TIME TO TRY THE FEEDER.

Loop to loop
Large loop
Bead
Link swivel
Cage Feeder

A GOOD BITE STRAIGHT AWAY! — THIS FEELS A MUCH BETTER FISH!

SURE ENOUGH, A BRIGHT EYED TENCH OF 3lb SCRAPS ALL THE WAY TO THE NET.

MARK SUGGESTS I FISH TOWARDS THE POINT OF THE ISLAND ON WAGGLER OR FEEDER.

ROY'S GOING TO FISH BOILIES TIGHT TO THE TREES ON THE ISLAND, FROM HIS SWIM BESIDE THE RUSHES.

THE LINE I'VE SETTLED FOR IS 40 YARDS OUT SO I'M FEEDING A GROUNDBAIT AND CASTERS MIX BY CATAPULT— LOOSE FEED WON'T GET ANYWHERE NEAR.

... NOW I'M LATCHING INTO A SUCCESSION OF SMALL, LIVELY CARP— COMMONS AND MIRRORS UP TO 2½lb.

AFTER A COUPLE OF BLEEPS ON HIS OPTONICS, ROY AT LAST GETS A BELTING RUN.

IT'S A TUBBY LITTLE COMMON OF AROUND 6lb — NOT A BIG FISH FOR THIS VENUE, BUT GAVE A GOOD ACCOUNT OF ITSELF ALL THE SAME.

THE SUN IS HIGH NOW AND I'VE HAD TO CAST MUCH TIGHTER TO THE ISLAND COVER TO FIND THE FISH. *THEY'RE COMING THICK AND FAST!*

I'VE GOT OVER 30lb OF FISH NOW— SMALL CARP, BREAM, TENCH AND ROACH— NOT BAD FOR A MORNING'S FISHING. MARK INSISTS THAT HE'S GOT SOMETHING EVEN BETTER IN STORE FOR THIS AFTERNOON ON ANOTHER SMALLER LAKE A FEW MILES AWAY ACROSS THE ESTATE.

Broadlands Fishery Continued

● It's possible to get a glimpse of the carp action at Broadlands from the fast lane of the M27 – and that is probably one of the reasons for its success. But good communications are only part of the story. Shrewd management and stocking have kept the day ticket rods rolling in. It all helps compensate for the decline of the salmon on the Test – thank goodness for carp runs!

I HAVEN'T GOT A GREAT DEAL OF TIME SO I'M GOING TO CONCENTRATE ON THE POLE, ON THE NARROW SIDE OF THE ISLAND. THERE'S PLENTY OF FISH TOPPING AGAINST THE ISLAND, SO I'LL TRY TO ENTICE THEM OUT RATHER THAN DUMP MY TACKLE ON TACKLE ON THEIR HEADS.

AFTER SPENDING THE MORNING ON THE MAIN LAKE AT BROADLANDS, I'VE DRIVEN TO ANOTHER PART OF THE ESTATE TO TRY THE NEW LONGBRIDGE FISHERY. THERE'S ABOUT 25 SWIMS, NOT A BIG WATER, BUT I'M ASSURED BY FISHERY MANAGER MARK SIMMONDS IT'S SOLID WITH FISH.

THE SWIM IS BUBBLING WITH FISH. THE MORE FEED I PUT IN, THE FASTER MY HOOK-BAIT IS SNAPPED UP! THIS IS A MORE NORMAL LAKE FISH, A 1lb SKIMMER.

FISHING SLIGHTLY OVERDEPTH, I'M STARTING TO MISS A LOT OF BITES. I THINK THEY'RE FALSE INDICATIONS CAUSED BY FISH KNOCKING INTO MY LINE.

I'VE HOOKED ONE AND IT'S A 1lb GOLDEN ORFE, THE FIRST TIME I'VE CAUGHT ONE OF THESE BEAUTIFUL FISH.

TEN MINUTES LATER AND I'VE TAKEN EIGHT GOLDEN ORFE BETWEEN 12oz AND 1lb .... NOW THEY'VE MOVED OFF.

THAT'S DIFFERENT A RAINBOW TROUT, TAILWALKING MY ELASTIC TO FULL STRETCH.

NOTHING FANCY, TACKLE WISE:

SMALL BODIED POLE FLOAT WITH FIBREGLASS STEM

2 Nº 4s

1·1lb HOOKLENGTH

Nº 11

1·7lb MAIN LINE

Nº 11

20 WHISKER BARB

I'M USING A MEDIUM ELASTIC BECAUSE I'VE BEEN WARNED THERE ARE SOME FAIR-SIZED FISH HERE. LOOSE FED MAGGOTS AND AN OCCASIONAL BALL OF CLOUDY BREADCRUMB SHOULD GET THINGS MOVING.

I'LL TRY SINGLE AND DOUBLE MAGGOT ON THE HOOK....

THAT DIDN'T TAKE LONG! FIRST CHUCK IN AND I'M INTO A POWERFUL FISH.

I WONDERED WHY MARK HAD A WRY GRIN ON HIS FACE WHEN HE SAID THIS SMALL LAKE WAS SPECIAL —— MY FIRST FISH IS A 1lb GRAYLING.

I TRY SHALLOWING UP AND HIT INTO A ROACH, TWO MORE GRAYLING, A CHUB, TWO SKIMMERS A BETTER 2lb BREAM AND TWO DACE.

THERE'S FISH TOPPING FOR MY LOOSE FEED NOW. I CONTINUE TO CATCH MORE SPECIES —— RUDD, GOLDEN RUDD, CRUCIAN CARP, COMMON CARP, MIRROR CARP, A COMMON GOLDFISH AND A FANTAILED ONE.

SUDDENLY MY SWIM HAS GONE ORANGE!

BITES ON TOP HAVE BECOME CAGEY NOW. I PUT IN SEVERAL HEAVY BALLS OF GROUNDBAIT LACED WITH A FEW CASTERS TO TRY AND GET THE FISH DOWN AGAIN. THIS WORKS IMMEDIATELY, FIRST A 1½lb BREAM, NOW SOMETHING MORE POWERFUL — A 2½lb TENCH, WHICH MAKES 15 DIFFERENT TYPES OF FISH IN TWO HOURS!

AN AMAZING LITTLE WATER!

JUNE
Met Police Pit
West Drayton, Middlesex

I'VE MADE A 5 a.m. START BECAUSE THE MAIN QUARRY ARE BIG TENCH. YOU DON'T SEE MUCH ACTION HERE IF YOU CAN'T GET THE FISH INTERESTED BEFORE THE SUN RISES TOO HIGH. HOWEVER, ONCE THEY'RE IN THE SWIM YOU CAN KEEP THE BITES COMING.

I'M TUCKED AWAY AT THE POINT OF THIS SECLUDED ISLAND ON LAKE TWO, THE SPECIMEN LAKE AS IT'S KNOWN, ON THE PRIVATE MET. POLICE FISHERY AT WEST DRAYTON.

ROY SETS UP TWO RODS WITH OPTONICS. HE'S FISHING POP-UPS TO AVOID THE BOTTOM WEED.

AH! THAT'S A PITY. PULLED OUT OF ANOTHER NICE TENCH THERE.

I'VE TRIED SHALLOWING UP TO ABOUT HALF DEPTH IN THIS 6ft DEEP SWIM AND I'M STILL GETTING THE BITES AND MISSING 'EM.

HIT THAT ONE THOUGH. THE FISH IN HERE REALLY GO!

I'VE PUT DOWN A CARPET OF RED EXPO GROUNDBAIT AND FED IN HALF A PINT OF HEMP AND THE SAME OF CASTERS OVER THE TOP. ALREADY THERE'S EVIDENCE OF TENCH ACTIVITY WITH MASSES OF TINY BUBBLES FIZZING AROUND MY WAGGLER FLOAT.

JUST AS 'MAIL EDITOR ROY WESTWOOD ARRIVES I'VE HIT INTO MY FIRST FISH, A GOOD TENCH BY THE WAY IT'S RUNNING.

A GOOD 4½lb FISH. THIS ONE TOOK DOUBLE CASTER ON A SPECIMEN EYED 18 HOOK TO 2·6lb HOOKLENGTH.

I TIE ON EYED HOOKS WITH A TYPICAL SPADE-END STYLE KNOT. MY REASON IS THAT WITH RELATIVELY FINE HOOKLENGTH BIG FISH LIKE TENCH CAN WEAKEN THE LINE WHERE IT LEAVES THE HOOK, PARTICULARLY WITH SPADE DESIGNS. THIS DOESN'T HAPPEN WITH EYED PATTERNS AS LONG AS THE HOOK IS WELL SUPPORTED WITH A KNOT DOWN ITS SHANK.

(7 to 10 TURNS)

EYED

SPADE

LINE PARTS HERE PARTICULARLY IF FISH DARTS INTO WEED

I'M GETTING BITES THICK AND FAST NOW BUT THEY'RE LIKE LIGHTNING. I'M HAVING EXTRA DIFFICULTY IN CONNECTING BECAUSE THIS SWIM'S A BIT OF A BIRDCAGE AND I CAN'T KEEP THE ROD LOW ON THE STRIKE.

IT'S ESSENTIAL TO FISH FINE HERE BECAUSE THE WATER IS GIN CLEAR. NORMALLY, MOST BITES COME BY FISHING JUST OFF THE BOTTOM OR ON-THE-DROP STYLE. IT'S ALSO IMPORTANT TO KEEP LOOSE FEED GOING IN ALL THE TIME.

ROY ALSO HAS MISSED SEVERAL SLOW RUNS ON HIS MINI BOILIE BAITS, BUT HE SUSPECTS THESE MIGHT HAVE BEEN CAUSED BY BREAM — FISH TO 8lb HAVE BEEN TAKEN HERE RECENTLY.

WONDER WHAT THIS IS? CERTAINLY NOT A TENCH BY THE WAY IT'S RUNNING.

WHILE DAVE PLAYS OUT THE MYSTERY FISH, SOMEONE IS SECRETLY WATCHING FROM THE HEAVILY OVERGROWN BANKSIDE SEVERAL HUNDRED YARDS AWAY.

Met Police Pit Continued

● The bottoms of gravel pits are often heavy on tackle. Line soon weakens when scuffed over bars and it's as well to run the last few feet between your fingers periodically to feel for abrasions. If there's a rough spot then take the trouble to retackle. Remember to store the discarded line carefully in your tackle box for safe disposal at home.

I'VE BEEN PLAYING THIS GOOD FISH FOR SEVERAL MINUTES ON LAKE TWO, PART OF THE PRIVATE MET. POLICE FISHERY AT WEST DRAYTON.

AFTER THAT CRUCIAN IT'S BACK TO MISSED BITES. TIME FOR A CHANGE TO THE LONG POLE.

THIS IS MY BIG TENCH POLE RIG. LATELY I'VE ONLY BEEN USING 2¼lb ELASTIC IN THE POLE INSTEAD OF THE WIDELY USED 4lb. I FIND THIS STRETCHES MORE. THE FISH HERE ARE SO BIG THAT YOU CAN GET BREAK-OFFS ON 1.7lb WITH THE THICKER GEAR.

FIBRE STEM BODIED POLE FLOAT WITH THICKISH TIP.

2.6lb

Nº4s

1.7lb

Nº11

Nº11

THAT'S INTERESTING. THERE'S A DEFINITE DEPRESSION IN THE BOTTOM ON 10½ METRES. I'LL CONCENTRATE ON THIS. I'M FISHING 10 METRES OR SO SHORTER THAN THE WAGGLER LINE.

I'VE PUT A COUPLE OF HELPINGS OF EXPO IN AND TOPPED UP WITH HEMP AND CASTER— ALREADY THE SWIM IS ERUPTING WITH BUBBLES.

THE FLOAT SUDDENLY SHOT AWAY! THIS IS A REALLY EXCITING WAY OF CATCHING TENCH! AND EFFECTIVE! I WOULDN'T HAVE CONNECTED WITH THAT BITE ON THE WAGGLER IN THIS AWKWARD SWIM.

THE SECRET WITH THE POLE AND LIGHT TACKLE IS TO GET THE FISH ON THE SURFACE BEFORE YOU START UNSHIPPING SECTIONS. OTHERWISE YOU END UP WITH 15 FOOT OF POLE AND 15 FOOT OF ELASTIC PLUS YOUR END TACKLE STRETCHING OUT OF CONTROL.

AN EVEN BIGGER TENCH!

WHAT'S THIS?! ROY WESTWOOD SAYS HE'S BEEN TO THE CARS TO FIND SOMEONE'S SMASHED HIS WINDOW AND TRIED TO RIP OUT THE RADIO!

THE POLICE HAVE BEEN CALLED. WHAT A PITY WE'LL HAVE TO CALL IT A DAY PREMATURELY, JUST WHEN IT WAS TURNING INTO A BRILLIANT SESSION. THESE FOUR FISH WEIGHED 20lb, THE BEST TENCH WAS 6½lb.

EARLIER I'D NOTICED A LONE FIGURE PERCHED ON A MOTOR BIKE IN THE DISTANCE. THE STRANGER IS STILL WATCHING EVENTS.

THIS IS A REALLY FINE FISH — A 3lb CRUCIAN CARP. JUST A COUPLE OF OUNCES SHORT OF THE LAKE RECORD I BELIEVE.

OH YES! THIS IS A REALLY BIG TENCH.

ABOUT 6lb, THAT ONE. THEY'RE REALLY GETTING THEIR HEADS DOWN TO THIS METHOD — HERE'S ANOTHER GOOD FISH. I'M REALLY IMPRESSED WITH THIS NEW 'FLY' POLE I'M TRYING OUT — IT'S TAKING A LOT OF STICK.

THE POLICE TAKE DESCRIPTIONS OF THE MYSTERY FIGURE ON THE MOTORBIKE. ROY'S CAR AND ANOTHER ANGLER'S ARE QUITE BADLY DAMAGED WITH ITEMS STOLEN. I'M LUCKY, MY ALARM HAS DETERRED THE THIEF FROM BREAKING IN.

AS WE'RE GIVING STATEMENTS TO THE POLICE THE BIKE RIDER IS SPOTTED IN THE DISTANCE. THE POLICE SET OFF IN HOT PURSUIT AND CALL UP REINFORCEMENTS.

SEVERAL POLICE CARS JOIN IN THE CHASE AND AN HOUR LATER THE BIKER IS ARRESTED AT ANOTHER LAKE. IN A MAD HOUR HE HAD BROKEN INTO SEVERAL OTHER ANGLERS' CARS. MOST OF THE STOLEN GEAR WAS RETRIEVED.

JUNE
River Trent
Sawley, Nottinghamshire

I'M STARTING ON THE OPEN-END FEEDER, DROPPING A WORM AND CASTER COCKTAIL BEHIND A LARGE BRANCH THAT'S SNAGGED IN THE MAIN FLOW. THERE SHOULD BE SOME GOOD FISH LYING IN THE SLACK WATER.

I'M FISHING ON THE MIDDLE TRENT IN NOTTINGHAMSHIRE WHICH MANY CALL THE MATCHMAN'S MECCA — MAINLY I SUSPECT BECAUSE IT'S STUFFED FULL OF FISH!

THAT'S BETTER! I AVOIDED THE WEED THAT TIME BY CASTING A BIT FURTHER OUT

PETE ARRIVES AND SHOWS ME HIS OWN MIDDY STICK FLOAT DESIGNS

PETE'S SETTLED DOWN IN A SHALLOWER AREA WITH MORE PACE, UPSTREAM FROM MY POSITION.

THAT DID THE TRICK! BY JUST HOLDING BACK AT THE END OF THE TROT THE TINY BLOB OF FLOAT LEFT SHOWING NUDGED UNDER AND A GOOD ROACH IS ON.

WHEN FISHING A STICK, SHIRT BUTTON STYLE, IT'S BEST TO CAST THE RIG OUT SO THAT THE SHOTS PRECEDE THE FLOAT IN A NEAT LINE. THEN HOLD BACK ON THE TACKLE UNTIL IT ARCS ROUND ONTO THE REQUIRED TROTTING LINE. IN THIS CASE PETE'S TROTTING JUST PAST THE ROD TIP IN 5 TO 6 FEET OF WATER.

IF YOU FEED CORRECTLY BITES OFTEN MATERIALISE ON-THE-DROP WHEN THE TACKLE IS CAST NEATLY AND SLIGHTLY HELD BACK.

River Trent Continued

● It is said that the most accomplished stick float anglers in the land did their apprenticeship on the Trent. But the days of roach duels and delicate float skills were rudely shattered when chub and barbel became more dominant. Then the swimfeeder increasingly entered the fray and changed the tempo of Trent matchfishing for all time.

HE LOSES THE PIKE AFTER A HECTIC BATTLE AND REELS IN A SEVERELY MANGLED ROACH.

TRENT STICK FLOAT MAESTRO PETE WARREN HAS HAD AN 8oz ROACH GRABBED BY A BIG PIKE AT THE TAIL END OF HIS SWIM.

I'VE MIXED UP SOME HEAVY GROUNDBAIT TO SEE IF I CAN GET THE FISH DOWN AND SORT OUT SOME BETTER ONES.

PETE'S HOOKED ANOTHER PIKE AND THIS TIME LANDS A FOUR POUNDER ON HIS FINE TACKLE.

THE EMERGING PATTERN SEEMS TO BE THAT THE TRENT IS TURNING BACK TO THE HEMP AND CASTER APPROACH, AFTER A COUPLE OF YEARS DOMINATED BY THE MAGGOT.

PETE ALSO FINDS TARES PULL THE ODD BETTER ROACH, BUT THEY ARE NOT WORKING CONSISTENTLY TODAY.

BUT ON THE POLE LINE THE NUMEROUS SKIMMERS AND SMALL ROACH WILL ACCEPT ANYTHING! I'M PROVING THIS BY CATCHING ON A WHOLE SPECTRUM OF BAITS OVER THE GROUNDBAIT.

HEMP   CASTER   TARES

MEANWHILE I'M STARTING TO CATCH SMALL ROACH AND SKIMMERS ON 9 METRES OF POLE.....

...USING A 1 GRAM BODIED POLE FLOAT WITH AN OLIVETTE RIG AND STYL WEIGHTS ON A 12oz HOOKLENGTH. MY SWIM IS SLOWER AND DEEPER THAN PETE'S.

SMALL STYL WEIGHTS

OLIVETTE

I'VE BEEN USING LOOSE HEMP AND CASTER FEED WITH MAGGOTS ON THE HOOK, BUT IN THIS DEPTH I'M GETTING PESTERED WITH SMALL FISH. A CASTER ON THE HOOK GETS SHELLED EVERY TIME.

THIS SEEMS TO SETTLE THE SWIM AND HE'S BACK ON THE ROACH.

BUT THE WEED PROBLEM IS STARTING TO AFFECT HIM TOO, AND HE LOSES AN ESTIMATED 2lb+ ROACH ON THE THICK NEARSIDE WEED AFTER IT MAKES A LAST DITCH PLUNGE FOR FREEDOM.

IT'S INTERESTING THAT PETE'S SO CONFIDENT IN HIS SHOTTING PATTERN HE ONLY THINKS IT NECESSARY TO MOVE HIS FLOAT POSITION TO KEEP IN CONTACT WITH THE FISH.

THERE'S NOT A GREAT DEAL IN IT BY THE TIME WE CALL IT A DAY. PETE'S PIKE HAS TIPPED THE BALANCE IN HIS FAVOUR, BUT HE'S IMPRESSED BY THE SMALL FISH CATCH I'VE PUT TOGETHER ...

...FROM THE DEEPER WATER WHERE THE TOP CURRENT MAKES HIS STICKFLOAT METHOD IMPOSSIBLE. IF HE DRAWS THIS AREA ON THE NEXT MATCH HE'S GOING TO FISH THE POLE

JULY
Linear Fisheries
Newport Pagnell, Buckinghamshire

Island   Island

carp moving

DAVE

ROY

WELL, I'VE GOT A FEELING I'M GOING TO HAVE A PASTING TODAY. I'M FISHING WITH ROY WESTWOOD AND FISHERY MANAGER LEN GURD ON POPLAR LAKE, PART OF THE LINEAR FISHERIES COMPLEX AT NEWPORT PAGNELL.

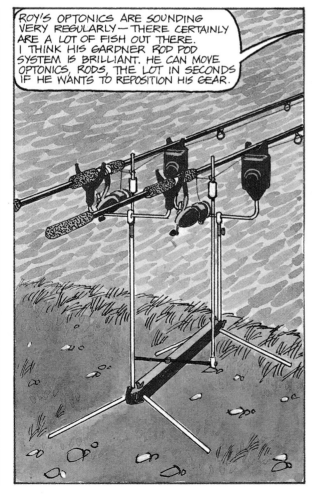

ROY'S OPTONICS ARE SOUNDING VERY REGULARLY — THERE CERTAINLY ARE A LOT OF FISH OUT THERE. I THINK HIS GARDNER ROD POD SYSTEM IS BRILLIANT. HE CAN MOVE OPTONICS, RODS, THE LOT IN SECONDS IF HE WANTS TO REPOSITION HIS GEAR.

THERE HE GOES AGAIN!

THERE'S A CANADA GOOSE NESTING JUST BEHIND THE BUSH ON THE ISLAND AND ROY'S GOT A SWAN NESTING OPPOSITE HIM. NEITHER BIRD HAS SHOWN ANY CONCERN — THE SWAN ACTUALLY CAME OVER TO US, LOOKING FOR TIT-BITS.

THOUGHT SO! LEN HAS PREBAITED WITH BOILIES AND ROY'S HOOKED A CARP STRAIGHT AWAY. I'LL HAVE TO WORK HARD TO GET THE FISH TO MOVE ONTO MY LOOSE FED MAGGOTS.

ROY NETS AN 8lb MIRROR THAT'S AS FAT AS A FOOTBALL, ON A STRAWBERRY FLAVOURED BOILIE.

I'M TUCKING MY 3AAA WAGGLER RIG AS TIGHT AS I CAN TO THAT OVERHANGING BUSH ON THE ISLAND, BUT ALL I'M GETTING IS SMALL ROACH EVERY CAST.

ROY'S HAD ANOTHER SMALL COMMON SO I'VE CHANGED TO SWEETCORN AND HOOK A GOOD FISH WHICH GOES TEARING OFF UNDER THE BUSH....

...EVEN WITH MY BEEFED UP TACKLE, THE FISH ZOOMED AWAY SO POWERFULLY THAT THE HOOK LOST ITS HOLD.

2·6lb
14 Drennan Specimen hook
Sweetcorn

A 7¾lb MIRROR THIS TIME.

I CAN SEE LEN IN THE DISTANCE PLAYING A GOOD FISH TOO.

LEN'S MIRROR WENT 11¼lb. NOW IT'S MY TURN, BUT THIS ONE DOESN'T FEEL THAT BIG..... A 3lb COMMON.

WE'VE MOVED OVER TO JOIN LEN ON ALDER LAKE. THERE'RE SOME GOOD CARP MOVING SO ROY'S GOING TO SETTLE HERE — I'VE GOT OTHER IDEAS.

LEN RECKONS THERE'RE SOME MONSTER BREAM AND ROACH HERE, SO I'M GOING TO FISH WELL OUT PAST THAT ISLAND.

Linear Fisheries Continued

● Fishery manager Len Gurd is an accomplished carp angler with a record of heavyweights second to none. But his skills as an artist and book illustrator are probably now more widely known. A great deal of the inspiration for his fish drawings arises from his daily observations at Linear as he walks the banks checking all is well — both with anglers and fish.

I'VE MOVED SWIMS AND SETTLED DOWN ON ALDER LAKE AT THE LINEAR FISHERIES COMPLEX AT NEWPORT PAGNELL. I'M FEEDING CASTER AND CHOPPED WORM OUT PAST THAT ISLAND, HOPING FOR SOME BIG BREAM.

A 20lb 6oz MIRROR IN PERFECT CONDITION.

ROY TOOK HIS FISH ON A POP-UP BOILIE FISHED ON A SEMI-FIXED BOLT RIG WITH DACRON HOOK LINK AND RIG TUBING.

THAT'S BETTER, A 12oz ROACH. I STILL HAD SOME OF MY BREAM GROUNDBAIT MIX LEFT AND THE BIGGER ROACH HAVE MOVED IN — PROBABLY THE CASTERS THAT DID IT.

MAGGOT, CASTER, IT DOESN'T MATTER WHICH I PUT ON THE HOOK, THE FISH ARE MOPPING UP THE BAIT AND I'M CATCHING QUITE A FEW ON THE DROP.

WHILE I'M GETTING AMONG THE ROACH LEN AND ROY RECKON THE BIGGER CARP HAVE MOVED BEYOND A SHALLOW BAR THAT'S COVERED WITH SHARP-EDGED SHELLS, AND CASTING TO THEM RUNS THE RISK OF WEAKENING THE LINE. THEY DECIDE THE RISK ISN'T WORTH TAKING.

ROY'S OPTONIC SOUNDS A SCREECHING RUN AND HE HITS A VERY GOOD FISH — THIS REALLY IS SOMETHING SPECIAL!

THE FAR SWIM HAS ONLY PRODUCED A COUPLE OF SMALL ROACH TO THE FEEDER SO I'VE MADE UP A WAGGLER RIG.

FISHING 4 ROD LENGTHS OUT I'M FINDING SMALL ROACH IMMEDIATELY BY LOOSE FEEDING MAGGOTS.

I'VE ONLY GOT ANOTHER COUPLE OF HOURS FISHING TIME SO I'M GOING TO GAMBLE ON PUTTING IN SOME GROUNDBAIT.

A NICE POUND FISH. I FOUND THIS ONE ON A MAGGOT AND CASTER COCKTAIL.

.... BUT THESE ROACH HAVE REALLY SAVED THE DAY— I'VE TAKEN 50 FISH UP TO THE POUND MARK. I'M IMPRESSED WITH THE FISHING AT LINEAR WHICH IS ONLY AN HOUR'S DRIVE UP THE M1 FROM MY HOME IN NORTH LONDON. I'LL BE BACK.

JULY
River Thames
Cookham, Berkshire

I'VE HAD A BIT OF A BARNEY WITH OUR CAPTAIN. HE'S CERTAIN THE MAGGOT FEEDER AND LONG POLE WILL DO MOST DAMAGE, BUT I RECKON THE OPEN-END FEEDER IS MILES BETTER ON THIS PART OF THE THAMES.

ESSEX COUNTY HAVE DRAWN COOKHAM IN THE D.F.D.S. CHALLENGE ON THEIR STRETCH OF THE MIDDLE THAMES AND WITH THE REST OF THE SQUAD I'M OUT PRACTISING FOR THE BIG DAY. NONE OF US REALLY KNOW WHAT TO EXPECT, BECAUSE THE COOKHAM STRETCH HAS BEEN PRIVATE FOR YEARS.

THE DROP-BACK OCCURS BECAUSE THE FEEDER IS JUST HOLDING BOTTOM AND ANY INTERFERENCE WITH THE HOOKBAIT DISLODGES IT.

2. FEEDER MOVES

3. CURRENT BOWS LINE BUT TENSION IS RELEASED

1. FISH PULLS ON HOOKLENGTH

4. TIP FALLS BACK

I THOUGHT THAT WAS AN EEL. YOU CAN TELL BY THE WAY THEY SUDDENLY STOP DEAD AND THUMP THE ROD TIP LIKE MAD.

THE BOATS HAVE STARTED TO MOVE AND BITES FADE. MAYBE THEY'VE PUSHED THE FISH FURTHER OVER – THERE'S 20 YARDS OF WATER TOWARDS THE FAR BANK, RELATIVELY UNDISTURBED. TO MY RIGHT, ANDY'S STRUGGLING ON THE MAGGOT FEEDER.

THERE'S ONLY ONE THING TO DO NOW AND THAT'S PUT OUT 6 MORE BALLS OF CASTER PACKED GROUNDBAIT INTO THE LESS DISTURBED AREA...

MAIN B

LONG POLE 10m. TO HAND

OPEN END FEEDER 60yd.

MAGGOT FEEDER 90yd.

I'VE GOT OUR TOP LONG RANGE MAGGOT-FEEDER ANGLER ANDY PARTRIDGE ON MY RIGHT AND LONG-POLE EXPERT GORDON BLANKS ON MY LEFT, (HE'S PILING IN MAGGOTS TOO.) I THINK I'M BEING SET UP.

I'M USING MY FAVOURITE CAGE FEEDER PACKED SOLID WITH HEMP AND CASTERS AND DOUBLE RED MAGGOT ON THE HOOK.

HAT'S HANDY! A GOOD TE FIRST CHUCK-IN AND A NICE 1lb SKIMMER.

I'VE GOT MY ROD POSITIONED QUITE HIGH AS THERE'S A LITTLE EXTRA FLOW. THIS KEEPS MORE LINE OUT OF THE WATER, ALLOWING ME TO FISH A LIGHTER FEEDER.

THE REWARD FOR FISHING MUCH LIGHTER AND FEEDING A SLIGHT BOW OF LINE INTO THE CURRENT IS BETTER BITE REGISTRATION, LIKE THIS CLASSIC DROP BACK.

AFTER A FEW TENTATIVE BITES I'VE TAKEN ANOTHER SKIMMER, BUT I'VE A HUNCH THERE'S A LOT OF FISH OUT THERE. I'M GOING TO TRY GIVING THEM FOUR MEDIUM BALLS OF GROUNDBAIT.

MEANWHILE, IN THE SWIM TO MY LEFT GORDON BLANKS IS SHOWING OFF HIS LONG-POLE-TO-HAND TECHNIQUE, TAKING SMALL DACE AND BONUS PERCH.

THIS FEELS BETTER. THE GROUNDBAIT HAS HAD A QUICK EFFECT AND I'VE TAKEN A 2lb BREAM.

CHANNEL

...BUT IT'S A NIGHTMARE TRYING TO AVOID THE BOATS. LOOK AT THAT! HE PULLED RIGHT ACROSS THE RIVER WITHOUT ANY WARNING AND MY GEAR'S HOPELESSLY SNAGGED ON THE RUDDER.

River Thames Continued

● There is free fishing on the Thames below Staines Stone and it's a fact that the biggest fish in the river are swimming in the bloodworm rich tidal reaches. Barbel of nearly 20lb and carp to more than 30lb are known to be present. Access is impossible to some of the most promising marks, particularly around Battersea.

MY THAMES PRACTISE SESSION WITH ESSEX COUNTY AT COOKHAM HAS BEEN RUDELY INTERRUPTED BY A BOAT. IT CUTS ACROSS MY LINE AND I LOSE THE END TACKLE.

A LULL IN THE BOAT TRAFFIC GIVES ME TIME TO EXPLORE THE QUIETER WATER FURTHER OVER. A SWITCH TO WORM AND CASTER ON THE HOOK AND I'M STARTING TO FIND 3 TO 4lb BREAM, EVEN TAKING THEM ON THE DROP.

IT'S INTERESTING THAT I'VE CAUGHT ONLY BREAM AFTER STARTING ON THE OPEN-END FEEDER, WHILE SOME OF MY TEAM-MATES HAVE PICKED UP THE ODD CHUB AFTER SWITCHING FROM MAGGOT. THE CHUB HAVE GONE FOR THE CASTER AND WORM BUT WERE COUGHING UP MAGGOTS. STRANGE!

I THINK I'D BETTER CALL IT A DAY. I'M BEGINNING TO AMASS A REALLY BIG WEIGHT— I'M NEARLY 30lb AHEAD OF EVERYONE ELSE! I WANT TO LEAVE SOME FISH FOR MATCH DAY IN CASE WE DRAW THIS PEG.

WE'VE DECIDED IT'S GOING TO BE THE OPEN-END FEEDER FISHED WELL ACROSS THE RIVER AS OUR MAIN LINE OF ATTACK AND TO FEED THE POLE LINE AS A RESERVE SHOULD THE FEEDER NOT WORK FOR EVERYONE. WE CAN'T BELIEVE HOW WELL THE RIVER IS FISHING— IS THERE A TRICK WE'VE MISSED?

POSTSCRIPT ON MATCH DAY ITSELF COOKHAM AND OURSELVES MAKE AN EARLY START TO MISS THE WORST OF THE BOAT TRAFFIC. PETE CLAPPERTON HAS CHOICE OF ODDS OR EVENS AS AWAY SIDE CAPTAIN AND PICKS EVEN PEGS. HIS CHOICE HAS SWUNG AGAINST ODDS, BECAUSE BIG WEIGHT PEG IS NUMBER 4 ON THE DAY.

THE MATCH TURNS INTO A BIT OF A STRUGGLE, AGAINST ALL EXPECTATIONS. TRAFFIC IS VERY BUSY AND TO ADD TO THE COMPETITORS PROBLEMS THERE'S A YACHT RACE ON THE VENUE TOO.

I DON'T MIND SHARING WATERS WITH OTHER INTERESTS, BUT SOME HOLIDAY BOATERS ARE GIVEN 2 MINUTES INSTRUCTION AND THEN LET LOOSE TO DO THEIR WORST. PITY THEY'RE NOT TAUGHT SOME WATER CRAFT.

AFTER ADDING SIX GOOD BREAM I'VE MADE MY POINT! CAPTAIN PETE CLAPPERTON HAS ORDERED HIS TROOPS TO SWITCH TACTICS WITH AMAZING RESULTS. APPARENTLY ALL THE SWIMS HAVE COME TO LIFE.

THAT BOATER KINDLY SLOWED DOWN WHEN HE SAW ME PLAYING A GOOD FISH. THANKS MATE!

THIS IS REALLY TURNING INTO A MARVELLOUS SESSION. THE MORE FEED I INTRODUCE, THE MORE FISH MOVE INTO THE SWIM. BIG SLABS SOME OF THEM TOO.

GORDON BLANKS HAS TAKEN OVER A HUNDRED FISH, MOSTLY DACE, ON THE LONG POLE FOR 10lb PLUS, BY FISHING A SHORT HOOKLENGTH AND ·70g OLIVETTE RIG. IT'S AMAZING HOW HE CASTS SUCH A LIGHT RIG SO SMOOTHLY ON A LONG LINE AND 10 METRE TELESCOPIC POLE.

IT'S A VERY CLOSE MATCH, IN THE BALANCE RIGHT TO THE DEATH, BUT MY METHOD DID PROVE INVALUABLE FOR ESSEX COUNTY TEAM MATE STEVE OROURK WHOSE BAG OF 9lb WAS TOP WEIGHT.

RESULT: ESSEX COUNTY 21·15·8
COOKHAM 20·9·0

AUGUST
River Severn
Diglis Weir, Worcestershire

I'VE STARTED ON THE STICK FLOAT, BUT I'M GETTING BLEAKED OUT, EVEN ON DOUBLE CASTER.

THIS IS THE FIRST TIME I'VE FISHED THE SEVERN. I'M BELOW DIGLIS WEIR AT WORCESTER WHICH HOSTS THE MACPHERSONS PAINTS MATCH TOMORROW, SO I'M GETTING IN A BIT OF PRACTISE.

MY FLOAT IS TILTING ALL OVER THE PLACE. THERE'S A LOT OF BLEAK OUT THERE.

..AND WHO SHOULD ARRIVE ON THE WATER BUT 'BORIS' HIMSELF! BIG FRANK SETS UP A STICK FLOAT RIG DOWNSTREAM.

THERE'S A WHO'S WHO OF FISHING LINING THE BANK HERE NOW...

WELL, I'VE TAKEN 5lb OF BLEAK VERY QUICKLY SO I'LL KEEP THIS METHOD IN MIND IF I DRAW AN EARLY PEG TOMORROW. THE BLEAK SEEM TO STAY AROUND HERE, WHICH IS PERMANENT PEG 26.

TIME TO TRY SOME TAKING METHODS. I'VE GOT ABOUT 7 ft. DEPTH ON THE 10 METRE POLE LINE BUT I'LL HAVE TO FIND A WAY PAST THE BLEAK.

BULK SHOTTING HASN'T SOLVED THE PROBLEM EITHER. THE BLEAK ARE SIMPLY FOLLOWING THE BAIT DOWN AND MY FLOAT REFUSES TO SETTLE.

ONLY ONE THING FOR IT—I'VE DECIDED TO GET A BLEAK RIG OUT AND SEE WHAT KIND OF WEIGHT IS ON THE CARDS WITH THESE TINY FISH.

IGNESTI BLEAKER FLOAT

ZZ FINE BARBLESS

10in 9½ OZ HOOKLENGTH

GROUP OF Nº II SHOT

FEEDING HALF A DOZEN MAGGOTS EVERY CAST, I'M CATCHING PLENTY OF BLEAK ON A 6 METRE POLE, BUT I SUSPECT I COULD CATCH EVEN QUICKER CLOSER IN.

I'VE SHORTENED THE RIG DOWN TO JUST 3 METRES AND BY INTRODUCING A LITTLE CLOUDY GROUNDBAIT I'M REALLY 'BAGGING UP' AS FRANK BARLOW WOULD SAY...

Terry Whichlon

... VAN DEN EYNDE ESSEX SKIPPER PETE CLAPPERTON HAS MOVED IN UPSTREAM.

...ENGLAND STAR BOB NUDD IS HERE

... AND THE 'RED MAN' JAN PORTER JUST STOPPED BY TO SAY HELLO.

I'VE TRIED MAGGOT ON A SHORT HOOKLENGTH BELOW AN OLIVETTE. THIS GETS THROUGH THE BLEAK BUT THE PRESENTATION ISN'T RIGHT.

OLIVETTE

10in

NOW I'VE SET UP A LONG HOOKLENGTH WITH 3 STYLS SPREAD BELOW THE OLIVETTE. I'VE BEEN FEEDING HEMP, SO LET'S GIVE THIS A GO.

OLIVETTE

3 Ft

SMALL STYLS

THE FLOAT DARTED UNDER FIRST TROT DOWN WITH A GRAIN OF HEMP ON THE HOOK, NOT A BAD SIZED FISH EITHER.

69

River Severn Continued

● Every barbel river in England appears to incite a similar record-breaking story. If all the reports are true, then salmon anglers have hooked record barbel on prawn or spinners from these waters during the Close Season. Just such a report circulated around the Severn — and there is every reason to believe it as double-figure specimens are on the increase.

A NICE ROACH.

I'VE JUST SWITCHED TO HEMPSEED ON THE LONG POLE BELOW DIGLIS WEIR AT WORCESTER AND A GOOD FISH IS HOOKED.

FRANK 'BORIS' BARLOW IS FISHING HIS FAVOURITE STICK FLOAT. HE'S BEEN CATCHING CHUB, NOW A BARBEL HAS PICKED UP HIS BAIT.

THAT WAS A SAVAGE TAKE! I FRACTIONALLY HELD THE FLOAT BACK AND IT FAIRLY SHOT UNDER— A GOOD FISH THIS ONE.

OH YES! A CRACKING ROACH.

NEARLY 1½ lb THAT FISH AND I'M STRAIGHT INTO ANOTHER.

NO CHANCE! THE HOOK'S PULLED FREE.

TIME TO TRY THE FEEDER I THINK, PACKED WITH HEMP AND CASTER.

MEANWHILE JAN PORTER IS SOON AMONG THE FISH A COUPLE OF SWIMS AWAY....

...THE MAN IN RED HAS A COUPLE OF CHUB ALREADY, NOW HIS MAGGOT FEEDER RIG HAS PICKED UP A 5lb BARBEL.

ESSEX COUNTY SKIPPER PETER CLAPPERTON HAS ALSO HOOKED A BARBEL, BUT HE'S IN BIG TROUBLE BECAUSE HE'S USING A POLE.

THE INEVITABLE HAPPENED WITH PETER'S BARBEL — IT PROVED JUST A LITTLE TOO POWERFUL FOR THE POLE. MEANWHILE I'VE TAKEN A COUPLE OF SMALLER ROACH ON HEMP. I'M TRYING A TARE ON THE HOOK NOW.

THE ROACH ARE COMING THICK AND FAST TO HEMP AND TARES.

5lb OF ROACH CAME VERY QUICKLY ON SEED BAITS THEN THE SWIM WENT STRANGELY QUIET. A SWITCH TO MAGGOT BROUGHT A FLURRY OF SMALL ROACH AND PERCH... FOR A SECOND I THOUGHT I'D HOOKED ANOTHER BIG ROACH BUT THIS IS STEAMING OFF LIKE A BARBEL.

I THOUGHT I'D HOOKED A BARBEL BUT IT'S A SMALL PIKE.

NOTHING ELSE HAPPENED ON THE FEEDER SO I'M PACKING UP. THERE'S DOUBLE FIGURES HERE — I HOPE I CAN DO THE SAME TOMORROW ON THE BIG MATCH! I'M OFF FOR A PINT OR TWO NOW WITH BORIS AND RIP-OFF.

AUGUST
River Derwent
Borrowash, Derbyshire

I'VE BEEN LOOKING FORWARD TO THIS TRIP ON THE DERBYSHIRE DERWENT FOR A LONG TIME. I'M FISHING WITH MIDLANDS MATCHMAN JAN PORTER.

I'M ALSO FISHING LIGHT BELOW THE FLOAT—TWO Nº 11 SHOT BELOW A 3 AAA INSERT WAGGLER. I TOOK A QUICK FLURRY OF SMALL CHUB ON CASTER, NOW I'M FINDING ROACH, MAINLY ON—THE—DROP.

20 KAMASAN WHISKER HOOK

NOW HE'S BACK ON THE FISHING SCENE WITH A VENGEANCE HAVING LED THE TRENTMEN SIDE TO DIVISION ONE SUCCESS ON THEIR HOME WATER.

THE DERWENT FISH SEEM TO WANT A LOT OF FEED. I'M REALLY STARTING TO BAG UP ON THE ROACH, FEEDING A HEMP AND CASTER MIX EVERY CAST AND FISHING SINGLE CASTER ON THE HOOK. I'M IGNORING ON—THE—DROP KNOCKS FROM SMALL STUFF AND LOOSE FEEDING AFTER I'VE CAST OUT TO TRY AND GET THE BETTER ROACH DEEPER DOWN.

... AFTER ALL, IT'S NOT EVERY DAY YOU GET BRILLIANT ROACH SPORT LIKE THIS !

JAN SEEMS TO BE DRAWING UP STREAMS OF SMALL CHUB FROM THE SHALLOWS BELOW HIM. HE HAS DECIDED TO SWITCH FROM MAGGOTS TO HEMP AND CASTER TO SEE IF HE CAN LURE SOME LARGER FISH WHICH ARE PROBABLY SHOALED HERE AFTER SPAWNING.

JAN HAS PICKED A NOTED CHUB PEG ON THE RUN-IN TO SHALLOWS. MY PEG HAS A MUCH STEADIER FLOW FROM THE MIDDLE OUT AND MORE DEPTH ON THE INSIDE LINE — LOOKS GOOD FOR ROACH.

FLOW

SHALLOWS

x x x

x x x

JAN'S USING ONE OF HIS OWN DESIGN MIDDY PEACOCK WAGGLERS...

...AND TO OVERCOME THICK BOTTOM WEED HE'S FISHING ON THE DROP.

2 SWAN LOCKING SHOT

21 90340 MUSTAD HOOK

FLOW

STYL

STYL

STYL

STYL

STYL

JAN'S TRADEMARK IN MATCH FISHING IS HIS COLOURFUL ALL-RED KIT. IT CERTAINLY DOESN'T SIGNAL DANGER TO THE FISH BECAUSE HE'S INTO SMALL CHUB ON MAGGOTS STRAIGHT AWAY! JAN GAVE UP FISHING FOR 6 YEARS TO PLAY LEAD GUITAR IN A ROCK GROUP.

THE CHUB ARE BOILING ON TOP IN JAN'S SWIM, SO HE LOOSE FEEDS MAGGOTS BEFORE CASTING TO LAND HIS BAITED HOOK AMONG THE EAGER FISH. IF HE CARRIES ON LIKE THIS JAN IS GOING TO GET AN IMPRESSIVE WEIGHT.

I'M GETTING THE ODD CHUB, BUT I DON'T THINK THERE ARE MANY IN THIS SWIM. IF I HAD STARTED ON MAGGOT I THINK I WOULD HAVE DRAWN A FEW MORE FISH UP FROM JAN'S SWIM, BUT I'LL STICK WITH THE ROACH' ON CASTER...

WELL THAT'S EXTRAORDINARY! THE FISH HAVE DISAPPEARED AS SOON AS THE HEMP AND CASTER WENT IN!

WHILE JAN SORTS OUT THAT ALARMING PROBLEM I'M SETTING UP A MIDDY PETE WARREN STICK FLOAT TO SEE IF I CAN BRING THE ROACH IN EVEN CLOSER.

River Derwent Continued

● Jan Porter's striking all-red kit is unique in angling but matching luggage and jackets bearing the names of sponsors have become all the rage in team fishing. Meanwhile, sombre colours remain standard issue in specimen hunting where camouflage rather than eye-catching colours are the priority.

AFTER A WHIRLWIND START WITH SMALL CHUB, JAN PORTER'S SWIM SUDDENLY DIED AFTER HE TRIED SWITCHING FROM MAGGOT TO CASTER FEED. MEANWHILE, I'VE CHANGED FROM THE WAGGLER TO A STICK FLOAT, CLOSER IN, TO TRY AND GROUP THE ROACH TIGHTER TOGETHER.

Nº 4
Nº 4
Nº 4
2 lb
Nº 4
1·1 lb
Nº 11   Nº 8

JAN SLOTS INTO THE PERFECT RYTHM, NOW HE'S GOT THE FISH IN A FEEDING FRENZY ON TOP. IT'S A CASE OF...

FEED

CAST

AND STRIKE EVERY TIME!

I'VE HAD AN EVENTFUL 1½ HOURS ON THE STICK FLOAT, TAKING 50 MORE QUALITY ROACH BUT I'M GOING BACK ON THE WAGGLER FOR THE FINAL MINUTES OF THE SESSION — I MUST TRY JAN'S STYL WEIGHT TRICK.

IT REALLY WORKS!

JAN FLINES IN MAGGOT LOOSE FEED AND THE SURFACE OF HIS SWIM ABSOLUTELY ERUPTS WITH CHUB AGAIN —— JUST AS THOUGH HE'D TURNED ON A TAP!

HE'S FINDING A BETTER STAMP OF FISH NOW. THE HEAVY FEEDING SEEMS TO HAVE GOT RID OF THE SMALL STUFF.

I'M ALSO INTO THE NEARSIDE ROACH. CAREFUL FEEDING OF HEMP AND CASTERS, HALF A DOZEN OF EACH EVERY CAST, IS DOING THE TRICK....

Tony Whieldon

...BUT THE TACKLE HAS TO BE RUN DOWN THE SWIM IN UNISON WITH THE LOOSE FEED TO GET A POSITIVE BITE.

SUDDENLY DISASTER STRIKES. HIS REEL LINE HAS TAKEN A HAMMERING AND PARTS AT THE REEL ON A GOOD FISH.

A BIT OF QUICK THINKING — HE PLUNGES HIS ROD INTO THE WATER AND TWISTS HIS ROD AROUND THE DISAPPEARING LINE.

HE MANAGES TO SNAG THE LINE AND LAND THE FISH ———

A 2 POUNDER

THE BEST ROACH OF THE DAY.

I'VE TAKEN 18–20lb OF PRIME ROACH, JAN'S DOUBLED THAT WITH CHUB. HIS RELAXED STYLE BELIES THE RATE HE'S CATCHING AT — A CLASS PERFORMANCE!

AUGUST
Lodge Pool
Farnham, Surrey

I'M GOING TO FISH THE WAGGLER AND BOMB, USING A MARKER LEFT BY A CARP ANGLER FOR MY FAR LINE FEEDING.

THIS SECLUDED DAY TICKET LAKE IN HAMPSHIRE LIES ON FORESTRY COMMISSION LAND AND IS CONTROLLED BY THE LOCAL FARNHAM CLUB. IT HOLDS PLENTY OF CARP, ROACH AND BREAM, BUT SPORT HAS BEEN VERY UNPREDICTABLE AND I DON'T KNOW WHAT TO EXPECT. THE SWIM I'VE CHOSEN IS AT THE POPULAR DAM END.

THERE'S SOME BIG CARP MOVING UNDER THE COVER TO MY LEFT, BUT NONE OF THE CARP ANGLERS HAVE HAD A RUN IN THE BRIGHT, WINDLESS CONDITIONS.

THAT DIDN'T TAKE TOO LONG. THE WATER IS QUITE COLOURED BUT I'M GETTING BITES QUICKLY ON CASTER — MUST BE A LOT OF FISH IN HERE.

I DON'T UNDERSTAND THIS. DESPITE PILING IN THE FEED I'M STILL NOT ATTRACTING ANY OF THE BIGGER FISH — EVEN THE SMALL ROACH ARE FADING FAST.

I'VE GIVEN THE FISH PLENTY OF TIME TO SETTLE ON THE FAR LINE SO LET'S TRY THE LEGER...

...LOOK AT THAT! — THE QUIVERTIP HARDLY HAD TIME TO SETTLE AND IT SOARED ROUND.

MARKER

10 RODS OUT
GROUNDBAIT, CASTER, SQUATT
(BOMB)

3 RODS OUT
HEMP AND CASTER
(WAGGLER)

THE LAKE IS VERY SHALLOW SO I'M ONLY FEEDING SMALL BALLS OF GROUNDBAIT, LACED WITH CASTER AND SQUATTS.

THE RIGS

13ft WAGGLER ROD

Nº12   Nº12s   Nº12s

18 FINE WIRE BARBLESS   1·7lb HOOKLENGTH   3 BB INSERT WAGGLER   2lb LINE

10ft 9in BOMB ROD

1·7lb HOOKLENGTH

18 FORGED BARBLESS   ½ oz BOMB   2·6lb LINE

...AS FOR THE WAGGLER, I'VE PUT DOWN A BED OF HEMP AND TWO POUCHES OF CASTERS. I'M FISHING WELL OVERDEPTH TO KEEP THE FISH FROM SEEING MY LINE GOING UP TO THE FLOAT.

FLOAT DRAWN WELL AWAY FROM FEED AREA

2·5ft   2ft

NOT MASSIVE, BUT NICE PLUMP 3-6oz FISH, THESE ROACH.

Tony Whieldon

I'M REALLY FIRING IN THE CASTERS NOW. THERE'S QUITE A LOT OF CARP ACTIVITY ON TOP AND PERHAPS BY FEEDING CONSTANTLY I'LL DRAW SOME IN.

IT'S NOT THAT BIG — A SKIMMER OF ABOUT 12 oz.

I FOUND A FEW MORE SKIMMERS, FISHING ON-THE-DROP WITH A 3 SWAN WAGGLER OVER THE GROUNDBAITED AREA, AND FINISHED THE STINT WITH ABOUT 7lb. DISAPPOINTING REALLY — THE BIGGER CARP, TENCH AND BREAM THE VENUE HOLDS FAILED TO SHOW.

THREE NORMALLY EFFECTIVE STILLWATER METHODS HAVE FAILED TODAY, BUT THIS GIVES ME A GOOD IDEA OF WHAT I WOULD DO IF I VISIT THE WATER AGAIN. I'M SURE A GOOD DOUBLE—FIGURE CATCH IS ON THE CARDS — IF I CAN FIND THE RIGHT METHOD.

SEPTEMBER
Royalty Fishery
Hampshire Avon, Christchurch

THE PARLOUR IS PROBABLY THE MOST FAMOUS SWIM ON THE HAMPSHIRE AVON'S ROYALTY FISHERY AT CHRISTCHURCH. THE POOL IS OFTEN FULL OF SALMON FRESH IN FROM THE SEA AND CONTAINS AT LEAST ONE BARBEL ESTIMATED AT 14lb AS WELL AS 3lb ROACH AND HUGE CHUB. YOU CAN'T FISH BEYOND THE CHAIN AND THAT'S WHERE MOST OF THE MONSTERS HIDE UP — THEY SWIM UNDER THE APRON, ALMOST BENEATH THE BUILDING ITSELF.

MOST OF THE FLOW IS COMING THROUGH ON THE FAR SIDE. I FANCY THERE COULD BE FISH JUST OFF THIS (A). THERE'S ALSO A NICE FLAT AREA IN THE CENTRE OF THE POOL — I'LL TRY HERE TO START WITH (B). MY PLUMMET ALSO TELLS ME THERE'S AN INTERESTING SPOT CLOSER IN, TO MY RIGHT, UNDER THE CHAIN (C).

FISHING ABOVE THIS LINE IS FORBIDDEN

MAIN FLOW

4ft   3½ ft   4ft 3in

(A)   (B)   (C)

FLOW FROM OLD SALMON PASS

MY FIRST FISH WAS A 1lb CHUB

ON THE FAR BANK, BELOW A WILLOW, RAY'S STARTED SEARCHING OUT THE WEEDY RUNS WITH LARGE CHUNKS OF LUNCHEON MEAT. HE USES 10lb STRAIGHT THROUGH TO A SIZE 2 LION D'OR HOOK.

RAY'S END RIG

THAMESLY SWAN SHOT

4-5in

ROUGHLY CUT LUNCHEON MEAT

RAY SIMPLY PINCHES SWAN SHOTS ON THE LINE UNTIL THERE'S JUST ENOUGH WEIGHT TO BOUNCE THROUGH THE SWIM. HE USES 10lb LINE BECAUSE HE'S DISCOVERED THE WEED HERE BREAKS AT 9lb PRESSURE. THE FISH FEEL SECURE IN THE WEEDY RUNS AND THE THICK DIAMETER LINE MAKES NO DIFFERENCE TO HIS CATCHES WHATSOEVER.

RAY'S KIT

A. TINS OF LUNCHEON MEAT— He uses four tins a session.

B. WATER PH KIT.

C. BINOCULARS.

D. WALKIE TALKIES.

E. CAMERA.

F. FRIARS BALSAM—which Ray brushes on sores or other damage on barbel — it helps them heal remarkably quickly.

G. AIR THERMOMETER.

H. WATER THERMOMETER

I. TAPE RECORDER — for making notes.

J. MEASURING TAPE.

K. SCALES.

MY COMPANION, RAY WALTON OF THE BARBEL CATCHERS, IS GOING TO FISH THE WEED-CHOKED STRETCH, BETWEEN THE PARLOUR AND THE MAIN RIVER, WHICH MOST ANGLERS WOULDN'T GIVE A SECOND GLANCE.
RAY HAS BEEN RESEARCHING THE ROYALTY BARBEL FOR SIX YEARS AND WAS RESPONSIBLE FOR EXPOSING THE PHENOMENON OF EXTRA WHISKERS. HE VIRTUALLY KNOWS EVERY SINGLE SPECIMEN ON THE ROYALTY BY SIGHT.

I THINK THESE PARLOUR FISH MUST SEE A LOT OF SPECIMEN GEAR. LET'S SEE HOW THEY RESPOND TO THE LIGHT APPROACH AND LOTS OF CASTERS.

I'M USING SANDVIK BULK SHOT IN CASE I GET A BIG FISH CHARGING OFF DOWNSTREAM INTO THE WEED. THESE WILL THEN POP OFF THE LINE LESSENING THE RISK OF A BREAK.

No.8 No.8 LIGNUM STICK
No.8 No.1s SANDVIK
No.8 1·7lb
18 FORGED BARBLESS

BY AIMING MY CATAPULT LOW I CAN GET THE BULK OF MY CASTERS IN THE MIDDLE, BUT THIS MAKES A FEW SKIM ACROSS THE SURFACE TOWARDS THE MAIN INFLUX OF WATER. THIS GIVES ME A GOOD AREA TO WORK WITH MY FLOAT TACKLE.

WEED
FLOW
FLOW — PATH OF FLOAT
ODD CASTERS FALL HERE
MAIN FEED

SOMETHING'S SNAPPED UP MY DOUBLE CASTER, OFFERING RIGHT AWAY!

RAY HOLDS HIS ROD ALL THE TIME, FEELING FOR BITES THROUGH THE LINE. HE LETS SLACK LINE REST ON THE WEED NOW AND THEN TO HOLD THE BAIT STILL — THEN TWITCHES IT SO THAT IT MOVES ON DOWN THE SWIM.

BACK AT THE POOL

I'VE HIT INTO SOMETHING BIG!

Royalty Fishery Continued

● Ray Walton's researches into barbel prove that some individuals travel long distances in a short space of time and by no means stay put in the area where they were first hooked. This nomadic tendency may be the result of angling pressure which is intense in some Avon swims where well known heavyweights are in residence.

I'VE BEEN PLAYING THIS FISH FOR SEVERAL MINUTES ON THE PARLOUR POOL ON THE HAMPSHIRE AVON AT CHRISTCHURCH. IT'S DARTING ALL OVER THE PLACE! SUDDENLY IT LIFTS IN THE WATER AND I SEE IT'S A COMMON CARP OF ABOUT 7 lb! IT'S TRYING TO GET INTO THE WEED TO MY LEFT NOW — I'M PILING ON THE SIDESTRAIN.

DAMN! THE FISH JUST TOUCHED THE WEED AND I FELT THE HOOK PULL OUT.

RAY INFORMS ME THE BARBEL WAS 4½ lb — THESE WALKIE-TALKIES ARE BRILLIANT WHEN YOU'RE FISHING WITH COMPANY. I THINK I'LL POP DOWN AND SEE HOW RAY IS FINDING THE BARBEL — THAT'S AFTER I'VE LANDED THIS NICE 2 lb PLUS CHUB.

....THEN RETURNS TO RUN THE BAIT THROUGH AGAIN. OFTEN HE FINDS A FISH THAT'S MISSED THE MEAL THE FIRST TIME, OR HAS BEEN SUSPICIOUS, DOESN'T LET HIS BAIT GO UNNOTICED NEXT TIME AROUND.

EVEN WITH QUITE A BIT OF SLACK IN THE LINE, SLIGHT PLUCKS FROM INTERESTED FISH ARE FELT QUITE POSITIVELY. *THAT WAS A KNOCK!*

RAY RECKONS MANY ANGLERS IGNORE SLIGHT KNOCKS LIKE THAT, THINKING THEY'RE CAUSED BY SMALL FISH, BUT HE KNOWS DIFFERENTLY. HE PRICKED A GOOD FISH THERE!

THIS IS RAY'S FAVOURITE BARBEL KIT. THE REEL IS TINY TO MY MIND, FOR THIS MODE OF FISHING, BUT HE FINDS IT SUPERB FOR HIS NEEDS.

11 Ft NORTH WESTERN MEDIUM SWIM FEED WITH BUILT-IN QUIVER.

10 lb MAXIMA OR SYLCAST

ROD REST INSERTED UP BUTT

SHAKESPEARE SIGMA GRAPHITE REEL

RAY OFTEN USES THE SPRING FROM A CLOTHES PEG AS WEIGHT INSTEAD OF THE MORE EXPENSIVE NON-TOXIC SHOT.

HIS HOOK KNOT IS INTERESTING. HE LEAVES PLENTY OF UNTRIMMED TAIL. THIS ALLOWS FOR SLIPPAGE IF HE HAS TO BULLY A BIG FISH OUT OF WEED.

HELLO! RAY WALTON IS COMING OVER ON THE WALKIE-TALKIE — HE'S GOT A BARBEL ON.

DOWNSTREAM, RAY LANDS HIS BARBEL.

RAY'S TECHNIQUE CERTAINLY IS AN ACTIVE WAY OF FISHING. HE'S CONSTANTLY ON THE MOVE. THE IDEA IS TO TRY AND RUN THE SOLITARY PIECE OF LUNCHEON MEAT RIGHT INTO THE FISH. IF THEY DON'T TAKE THE FIRST TIME HE RESTS THE SWIM FOR 15 MINUTES OR SO....

RUN

I'M FASCINATED WITH RAY'S APPROACH. HE OBVIOUSLY PUTS A GREAT DEAL OF THOUGHT AND EFFORT INTO HIS FISHING. ANYWAY, TIME TO SEE IF ANYTHING'S MOVED ONTO THE FEED I'VE BEEN PUTTING DOWN CLOSER IN AT THE PARLOUR. THIS SUSPENDED CHAIN IS A NUISANCE, THERE'S LOTS OF LOST TACKLE HANGING FROM IT.

YES! OH YES! THIS IS A GREAT FISH! FEELS LIKE A BIG BARBEL BUT YOU CAN NEVER BE SURE IN THE PARLOUR.

Royalty Fishery Continued

● Considerable controversy surrounds Ray Walton's discovery of the extra whiskers sprouted by many barbel on rivers as far apart as the Lea and Hampshire Avon. Some claim the phenomenon is not new but Ray is adamant that it demonstrates all is not well with their diet or possibly water quality.

WHAT A LOVELY FISH. RAY'S WEIGHED IT FOR ME AT 8lb 3oz — NOT BAD FOR AN 18 HOOK AND 1.7lb HOOKLENGTH!

I'VE BEEN PLAYING THIS FISH IN THE PARLOUR FOR 3 OR 4 MINUTES NOW.

I THINK IT'S A BIG BARBEL— IT'S A LOT SLOWER MOVING THAN THAT CARP I LOST.

YES IT'S A BARBEL— AND BY THE LOOKS OF IT MY PAN LANDING NET IS BARELY BIG ENOUGH.

I'M GETTING PLENTY OF BITES CLOSE IN TO MY BANK. I GET A RESPONSE IN THE SLACK OR IF I DRAG THE FLOAT ACROSS THE WATER FLOWING OUT FROM THE SALMON PASS.

SLACK

FLOW

FLOAT

HERE'S ANOTHER GOOD FISH....

.... A SUPERBLY CONDITIONED 4lb CHUB.

THAT'S ANNOYING. THE HOOK'S GONE. IT'S STRANGE BECAUSE MY TACKLE HAS BEEN STANDING UP TO THE OCCASION SO FAR. MIND YOU, I HAD TIED ON A NEW PATTERN I'D BEEN ASKED TO TRY OUT FOR REVIEWING PURPOSES.

LET'S HAVE A LOOK AT ANOTHER. NO WONDER— THE SPADES ON THESE ARE LIKE RAZORS! THAT LITTLE LOT CAN GO STRAIGHT IN THE BIN. NO REVIEW FOR THIS PRODUCT— THE SUPPLIER MIGHT WELL GET A STIFF LETTER THOUGH.

THIS IS BETTER. BACK TO MY OLD FAVOURITES AND NO PROBLEMS. STILL YOU'VE GOT TO BE FAIR AND TRY NEW PRODUCTS. I ONLY WISH A LITTLE MORE THOUGHT WENT INTO SOME OF THEM.

IT'S GOT AN EXTRA WHISKER ON THE REAR BARBULE AND RAY MAKES A CAREFUL NOTE OF ITS LENGTH. I WONDER WHAT'S REALLY CAUSING THESE EXTRA GROWTHS?

BACK IT GOES IN THE SLACKER WATER. I'LL HOLD IT UPRIGHT FOR A MINUTE UNTIL IT CAN SWIM AWAY UNDER ITS OWN STEAM.

I'LL ONLY KEEP THE CHUB IN MY KEEPNET TODAY — BARBEL MUST GO STRAIGHT BACK. THERE GOES THE WALKIE TALKIE AGAIN! RAY'S INTO ANOTHER FISH AT THE BOTTOM OF THE SHALLOWS, DOWNSTREAM OF THE PARLOUR POOL.

IT'S ANOTHER GOOD BARBEL HOOKED FROM RIGHT UNDERNEATH THE WILLOW ON THE FAR BANK.

RAY LANDS THE FISH AND CAREFULLY WEIGHS IT AT 7lb 2oz. HE LOGS THE DETAILS DOWN METICULOUSLY AND PHOTOGRAPHS THE FISH.

I'M ALSO IN THE THICK OF IT AGAIN WITH A LIVELY SEA TROUT.

THIS IS BRILLIANT. ANOTHER BIG CHUB BY THE FEEL OF IT!

IT PROVED TO BE YET ANOTHER 4 POUNDER AND NOW I'VE HOOKED A BARBEL.

AH! THE FISH SEEMS TO HAVE COME OFF.

HERE'S MY BEST THREE CHUB — ALL 4 POUNDERS. I'VE ALSO TAKEN SEVERAL SMALLER SAMPLES, THAT 8lb BARBEL AND THE SEA TROUT.

IT'S GETTING DARK AND RAY HAS MOVED UP TO FISH THE LAWN SWIM AT THE END OF THE PARLOUR — HE'S GOT SOMETHING ON!

RAY TELLS ME ON THE WALKIE TALKIE THAT IT'S A 9lb 11oz BARBEL — ANOTHER FISH FROM HIS LOGBOOK OF CATCHES. WHAT A GLORIOUS WAY TO END OUR DAY IN THE PARLOUR.

SEPTEMBER
Exeter Canal
Lime Kilns, Devon

I'VE GOT ROB ROYCE OF BRIDGWATER WITH ME TODAY. HE WON A COMPETITION, EARLIER IN THE YEAR, TO APPEAR IN MY DIARY AND WE'VE DECIDED ON A SESSION AT THE LIME KILN STRETCH OF THE EXETER CANAL. ROB'S HOME WATERS IN SOMERSET ARE THE BRIDGWATER CANAL AND HUNTSPILL. HE'LL FIND THIS VENUE A LOT DEEPER. I LIKE HIS HAT!

A MATCH WAS WON ON PERMANENT PEG 119 — BY THE SEWAGE BARGE — BUT WE FANCY THESE WIDER SWIMS IN FRONT OF THE CAR PARK.

TO RING THE CHANGES LATER ON I'VE SET UP A LONG POLE RIG TO FISH 14ft DEEP. I'LL FLICK SOME HEMP AND MAGGOTS OUT REGULARLY AND TRY THE POLE AT ODD INTERVALS TO SEE IF ANYTHING MOVES IN.

IT DIDN'T TAKE LONG FOR A BITE, BUT THAT'S THE ONLY TROUBLE WITH SMALL BAITS — A TINY PERCH HAS SNAPPED UP THE OFFERING.

THAT'S A BETTER ONE! A COUPLE OF TINY TWITCHES ON THE QUIVERTIP AND I STRIKE INTO A PLEASING 12 oz SKIMMER.

I'M USING MY SLACK LINE TECHNIQUE NOW — LETTING THE LINE BOW INTO THE DRIFT TO SEE IF THIS DRAWS A MORE POSITIVE TAKE.

MEANWHILE BOB'S STRUGGLING. HE'S TRIED THE SWINGTIP AND THE WAGGLER BUT ONLY HAD A SMALL PERCH SO FAR.

AS FOR ME I'M HITTING INTO SKIMMER AFTER SKIMMER.

BARGE   BARGE

I'LL START ON THE OPEN-END FEEDER. IT'S VERY WEEDY ON THE FAR BANK SO I'LL CONCENTRATE JUST PAST THE MIDDLE WHERE IT SEEMS CLEARER. I'M HOPING TO FIND THE LIME KILN'S SKIMMERS.

18in loop   1lb hooklength

Bead

3lb reel line   American link swivel   Cage feeder   20 Whisker barb

1 Gram wire stem bodied pole float

1·5 Main line

Olivette

Styl
9½ oz hooklength
Styl

22 series 4 Tubertini

MY HOOKBAIT IS TWO PINKIES WHICH ARE NICE AND SOFT — SKIMMERS TAKE THEM WELL. IN THE FEEDER, I'VE PACKED A MIXTURE OF HEMP, CASTERS AND SQUATTS IN A MINIMUM OF SOFT GROUNDBAIT. THE SQUATTS WILL PULL ANYTHING AROUND WHILE THE CASTERS WILL HOLD ANY BETTER FISH.

YES! WITH LESS RESISTANCE THE TIP WENT ROUND.

A BETTER SKIMMER, JUST OVER THE POUND MARK.

I'VE GOT THE FEEDER MIX JUST RIGHT. THE FEED'S COMING OUT AS THE FEEDER HITS ...

..AND THE SKIMMERS ARE HOMING IN ON-THE-DROP. NINE SKIMMERS UP TO A POUND IN THE NET ALREADY.

Exeter Canal Continued

● The wide and deep reaches of the Exeter Canal have become familiar to matchmen throughout the country as a popular Close Season series has been promoted on the water in recent years. The Lime Kilns is now nationally known for its bream potential.

MAIL READER ROB ROYCE IS FISHING WITH ME ON THE EXETER CANAL, BUT HIS SWIM ISN'T PRODUCING THE GOODS....

I THINK THE GENTLE LOOSE FEEDING WASN'T POSITIVE ENOUGH IN THIS DEPTH OF WATER. I WAS GETTING ODD KNOCKS ON THE DROP— NOW I'VE CONCENTRATED THE FISH ON THE BOTTOM AND THEY'RE REALLY SNAPPING UP MY SINGLE MAGGOT HOOKBAIT.

I'M STILL GETTING BITES FROM THE ROACH ON-THE-DROP BY LOOSE FEEDING MAGGOTS OVER THE GROUNDBAIT, BUT THE FISH ARE A LOT DEEPER DOWN AND I'M CONNECTING WELL.

THIS IS A BETTER FISH IT'S PULLING A FAIR BIT OF ELASTIC FROM THE TIP OF MY POLE. I MANAGED TO AVOID A BITE ON-THE-DROP THAT TIME AND SETTLED MY HOOKBAIT ON THE BOTTOM FOR A COUPLE OF MINUTES.

ROB'S BEEN TRYING SOME OF MY GROUNDBAIT MIX IN HIS FEEDER AND FINALLY GETS A BITE, BUT THE EXCITEMENT IS SHORT LIVED — IT'S ONLY A TINY BOOTLACE EEL!

I EXPERIMENT BY SHORTENING MY RIG BUT IT ONLY BRINGS SMALL ROACH.

BACK HARD ON THE BOTTOM AGAIN AND THE BREAM ARE READY AND WAITING.

...BUT I'M IN LUCK FURTHER ALONG THE BANK. MY LIGHT MATCH FISHING APPROACH HAS BUILT UP A GOOD NET OF 12oz – 1lb SKIMMERS ON THE OPEN-END FEEDER. IT'S TIME FOR A SWITCH TO THE LONG POLE TO SEE WHAT'S ON THE INSIDE LINE.

INSTANT SUCCESS WITH A BITE FIRST CAST!

THAT'S ODD! AFTER LANDING ONE SOLID ROACH AND A SMALL PERCH, THE SWIM DIES. I'D HAVE THOUGHT MY PATIENT FEEDING OF MAGGOTS AND HEMP DESERVED MORE.

LET'S TRY GIVING 'EM SOME. I'VE QUICKLY MADE UP SOME EXTRA GROUNDBAIT AND MIXED IN SQUATTS AND CASTERS. SIX ORANGE-SIZED BALLS SHOULD DO.

AMAZING! THAT LITTLE LOT BROUGHT THE FISH IN AS IF BY MAGIC.

A NICE SKIMMER OF A POUND.

A TIDY NET OF SKIMMERS AND ROACH WELL INTO DOUBLE—FIGURES. ROB'S ENJOYED HIS DAY AND WE'VE ENJOYED HIS COMPANY.

TIME TO GO NOW. IT'S A LONG HAUL BACK TO LONDON FOR ME. PITY IT'S SO FAR OR I'D BE BACK LIKE A SHOT FOR THE WEEKEND MATCH.

OCTOBER
River Thames
Pangbourne, Berkshire

MY RIG MAY LOOK COMPLICATED BUT IT'S THE BEST LONG RANGE ANTI-TANGLE SYSTEM I'VE EVER DISCOVERE[D]

4lb REEL LINE

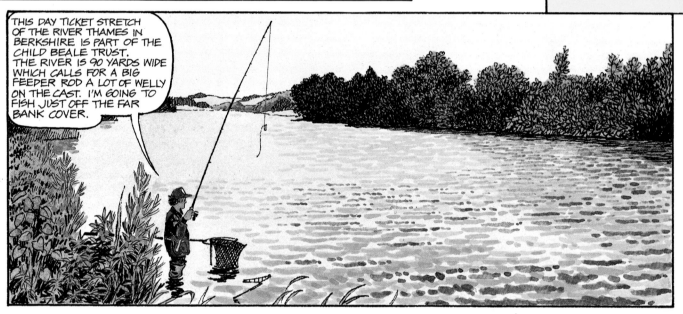

THIS DAY TICKET STRETCH OF THE RIVER THAMES IN BERKSHIRE IS PART OF THE CHILD BEALE TRUST. THE RIVER IS 90 YARDS WIDE WHICH CALLS FOR A BIG FEEDER ROD A LOT OF WELLY ON THE CAST. I'M GOING TO FISH JUST OFF THE FAR BANK COVER.

I'M NOT CASTING TOO TIGHT AT THE START— IT'S BETTER TO SEE IF FISH CAN BE ENCOURAGED OUT FIRST.

SUNKEN WEED

ORDINARY MAGGOTS IN THE FEEDER PRODUCED NO RESULTS, BUT IN THE MEANTIME I'VE BEEN SOAKING SOME MAGGOTS IN WATER TO MAKE THEM FLOAT. LET'S TRY A FEW IN THE FEEDER AND A COUPLE ON THE HOOK.

GREAT TIP FOR WET MAGGOTS NEW ESCAPE-PROOF BAIT BOX FROM EAST ANGLIAN ROD CO.

YOU GET WEIRD SENSATIONS AT TIMES, WHEN FEEDER FISHING AT LONG RANGE. AT FIRST THIS FISH FELT LIKE A HALF-POUNDER, BUT AS I'VE BROUGHT IT NEARER IT HAS GOT 'BIGGER'. FISH LIKE CHUB OR BREAM OFTEN FOLLOW THE FEEDER IN MEEKLY, THEN EXPLODE INTO ACTION WHEN THEY SEE THE ROD.

A NICE 2lb CHUB.

NEXT CAST AND A FISH NEARLY TOOK THE ROD OUT OF THE RESTS . . .

12in LOOP

3in LOOP

½in LOOP ½in LOOP

1.7lb HOOKLENGTH

16 FORGED HOOK

FREE RUNNING BEAD

DRENNAN FEEDERLINK

BLACK ELECTRICAL TAPE MASKING LOWER HOLES TO RESTRICT FLOW OF MAGGOTS

¾ OR 1oz WEIGHT

THE 12in LOOP GIVES ENOUGH RUN FOR A TAKING FISH TO REGISTER ON THE QUIVERTIP.

THE 3in LOOP PREVENTS THE SMALLER LOOPS FROM TANGLING AROUND THE FEEDERLINK.

THE BEAD PREVENTS THE BASE KNOT FROM SNAGGING IN THE LINK'S EYE.

SMALLER LOOPS ALLOW FOR LOOP TO LOOP ATTACHMENT OF THE HOOKLENGTH TO THE REEL LINE. THESE LOOPS ADD ENOUGH RIGIDITY TO KEEP THE HOOKLENGTH FROM WRAPPING AROUND THE FEEDER.

I SEE A LOT OF ANGLERS MESSING AROUND WITH SEVERAL EXTRA SIDE LEADS AND SHOCK LEADERS WHEN TRYING TO GAIN DISTANCE, BUT COMBINE THE RIGHT WEIGHT WITH THE RIGHT LINE AND A GOOD ROD AND YOU CAN FISH A LOT LIGHTER WITHOUT FEAR OF BREAK-OFFS ON THE CAST.

FLOATING MAGGOTS MAKE THE HOOK SINK A LOT SLOWER AND OFTEN DRAW FISH INTO THE SWIM— THEY CERTAINLY EXCITE THE FISH.

LOOK AT THAT! ALMOST IMMEDIATELY THE TIP WENT ROUND AND I'M INTO A FISH.

...THAT WAS ANOTHER 2-POUNDER AND I'M INTO A THIRD FISH ALREADY! I GET THE FEELING THERE'S A LOT OF FISH OUT THERE, BUT I'LL HAVE TO STOP USING FLOATING MAGGOTS FOR A WHILE AS THE CHUB ARE CHASING THEM DOWN RIVER, OUT OF THE SWIM.

River Thames Continued

● Heavy boat traffic in summer poses problems for anglers right along the Thames and at weekends it can become unbearable. The congestion is unlikely to ease and the need to develop stillwater venues exclusively for fishing is now regarded by many in the sport as the only salvation. Luckily, there are many hundreds of acres of pits in the Thames Valley where you can escape.

AFTER TAKING THREE CHUB IN QUICK SUCCESSION, THE PLEASURE BOATS INTERRUPT MATTERS. THAT'S THE TROUBLE WITH THIS LONG RANGE FEEDER METHOD — YOU SOMETIMES HAVE TO WAIT SEVERAL MINUTES BEFORE RECASTING BECAUSE OF BOAT TRAFFIC.

THE BOATS TEND TO PUSH THE FISH TIGHTER IN TO THE FAR BANK, BUT ON THE OTHER HAND THE REST CAN DO THE SWIM GOOD. ON BALANCE IT'S BETTER TO SIT IT OUT WITHOUT A BAIT IN THE WATER BECAUSE IF A PROPELLER CATCHES THE LINE IT COULD ALMOST EMPTY THE SPOOL.

THE APPEARANCE OF THE PERCH IS FOLLOWED BY A STRANGE LULL — I WONDER WHAT'S HAPPENED TO THE CHUB?

Tony Whieldon

A FEEDER CRAMMED WITH FLOATING MAGGOTS BROUGHT THE FISH BACK STRAIGHT AWAY. THERE'S NO DOUBT IN MY MIND THAT FLOATERS CAN TRANSFORM A SWIM — THE RUSE HAS WORKED MANY TIMES ON THIS STRETCH OF THE RIVER, AND ELSEWHERE.

I LOST THAT FISH TOO, SO I'M GOING TO TRY RAISING THE ROD ABOVE MY HEAD TO GET THIS ONE OVER THE SNAG.

THAT'S BETTER. THE CHUB STAYED UP IN THE WATER AND I'VE GOT IT TO THE NET.

MY TWO BEST FISH ARE A POUND PLUS PERCH AND THE 3lb CHUB. AFTER THREE HOURS I'M WELL ON MY WAY TO 20lb, WITH EIGHT CHUB ALTOGETHER. UNFORTUNATELY I'VE GOT TO LEAVE NOW, JUST WHEN THE FISH ARE LINING UP. BUT THAT'S LIFE!

OCTOBER
River Lea
Stonebridge Lock, London

CASTER FEED

BROKEN REMAINS OF SUNKEN BARGE

FAR BANK SHELF 2-3 FT

MAIN BOAT CHANNEL 6-7 FT

STONEBRIDGE FISHES BRILLIANTLY FOR CHUB AND I'VE PICKED A HOT-SPOT KNOWN AS THE SUNKEN BOAT PEG. TH WRECK LIES ALONGSIDE THE FAR BANK AND BI CHUB LIVE INSIDE IT. I'M FEEDING CASTERS, HOPING TO DRAW SOME OF THEM OUT.

NEARSIDE SHELF 4-5 FT.

IT'S 6 a.m. AND I'M HOPING FOR GREAT THINGS TODAY ON MY FAVOURITE STRETCH OF THE CANALISED LEA AT STONEBRIDGE LOCKS, JUST A MILE DOWN THE ROAD FROM MY NORTH LONDON TACKLE SHOP.

IT'S DIFFICULT TO FISH NEAR THE BOTTOM IN THIS SWIM. THERE'S MANY MORE SNAGS AROUND THE SUNKEN BOAT THIS SEASON AND I'M FINDING 'EM!

WHEN I MANAGE TO STEER CLEAR OF THE SNAGS, SMALLER CHUB AND DACE SNAP UP THE HOOKBAIT ON-THE-DROP.

I'VE BEEN FEEDING A FEW GRAINS OF HEMP REGULARLY ON THE NEARSIDE — THINK I'LL GIVE THE POLE A GO ...

... THE ROACH ARE THERE STRAIGHT AWAY.

Nº 3 OLIVETTE

STYLS

18 BLUE GAMAKATSU

THIS IS MY FAVOURITE FAR BANK CHUB RIG FOR THE VENUE — IT HAS WON ME A LOT OF MATCHES HERE.

2·5 MAXIMA

SMALL SWIVEL

1·7 BAYER

SMALL STYL

SIZE 18 DRENNAN CARBON BARBLESS

3AA + DRENNAN CRYSTAL WAGGLER

DINSMORE Nº 4s

SSG   AAA
(SANDVIK)

THE SWIVEL IS VERY IMPORTANT — IT PREVENTS THE DOUBLE CASTER HELPING FROM SPINNING UP THE HOOKLENGTH ON THE RETRIEVE. IT ALSO ACTS AS A BRAKE, CATCHING ON THE FINE BOTTOM WEED AND ANCHORING THE FLOAT IN THE DRIFT.

AS THE SUN RISES OVER LONDON I MAKE MY FIRST CAST TO THE FAR BANK AND IMMEDIATELY HOOK A CHUB.

THESE CANAL CHUB PUT UP A HECK OF A FIGHT! THIS ONE'S ONLY ABOUT A POUND BUT IT DOESN'T WANT TO KNOW THE LANDING NET.

THE BETTER FISH ARE DEEPER DOWN. I'VE JUST CONNECTED WITH A VERY GOOD CHUB BUT IT DASHES INTO THE SUNKEN BOAT AND RUNS ME INTO A SNAG. THESE CHUB ARE MASTER ESCAPOLOGISTS — THEY RARELY BREAK YOU, BUT OFTEN MANAGE TO TRANSFER THE HOOK INTO SOMETHING SOLID.

AFTER TAKING A FEW ROACH THE SWIM SUDDENLY GOES DEAD. I TRY A CASTER ON THE HOOK AND THE POLE IS NEARLY SNATCHED FROM MY HANDS!

River Lea Continued

● There's a great irony attached to this story of Dave's session in the sunken barge swim. He returned to the same spot a few days later and found no sign of the wreckage on the far bank. It had been removed – presumably by British Waterways – and with it had gone the chub shoals!

"I'D LIKED TO HAVE SEEN WHAT THAT WAS! I'VE LOST A FEW MYSTERY BIG FISH ON THE POLE ON THIS VENUE RECENTLY. COULD HAVE BEEN A BIG CHUB, OR PERHAPS A CARP. IT'S RUINED MY INSIDE LINE – SO BACK TO THE WAGGLER."

"I'VE TAKEN A COUPLE OF SMALL CHUB AND A PAIR OF HERRING-SIZED DACE FROM THE BOAT. I'VE ALSO HIT INTO A COUPLE OF BIG FISH WHICH HAVE SNAGGED THE TACKLE ALMOST IMMEDIATELY. THERE'S LOADS OF LOST LINE OUT THERE – THE SWIM IS ALMOST UNFISHABLE COMPARED TO LAST SEASON'S FORM."

"THE CLEARER AREA TO THE LEFT OF THE WRECK IS ALIVE WITH SMALL CHUB AND DACE, BUT NO SIGN OF 3 OR 4 POUNDERS."

"I CAN VIRTUALLY PICK UP A ROACH A CHUCK NOW – AND SOME PEOPLE SAY THIS IS A BLOODWORM VENUE."

"I SUSPECT THE TRUTH OF THE MATTER IS THAT ANGLERS ARE MORE PREOCCUPIED WITH THE CONTROVERSIAL BAIT THAN THE FISH. I'VE HAD A 1st AND 2nd IN THE LAST TWO MATCHES HERE FISHING CASTER AND HEMP."

"I DON'T BELIEVE IT. I'VE HOOKED ANOTHER OF THOSE MYSTERY FISH!"

I'VE HOOKED SOMETHING REALLY BIG ON THE POLE WHICH FORCES ME TO ADD EXTRA SECTIONS TO KEEP IN CONTACT.

THEN DISASTER

THE HOOK'S LOST ITS HOLD!

FIRST FEED AREA

A

B

SUNKEN BOAT

UNDERWATER SNAGS

I'VE FORMED A MENTAL PICTURE OF WHERE THE SNAGS ARE LOCATED AND MY FIRST FEED AREA WAS A MISTAKE. I'VE BEEN FEEDING AREAS A AND B WHILE TRYING THE POLE.

I'VE STEPPED UP MY TACKLE AND I'M GOING TO TRY FISHING INSIDE THE WRECK. IF I HIT ANYTHING BIG IT'S GOING TO BE TOUCH AND GO, BUT IT'S WORTH THE RISK AS THE REWARD CAN BE A 4lb PLUS FISH HERE.

I THINK THE BRIGHT, EARLY MORNING SUN HAS MADE THE QUALITY CHUB RELUCTANT TO LEAVE THEIR LAIR. I RECKON SOME OF THE EASIER TO FISH SWIMS WOULD STILL HAVE PRODUCED WELL BUT I WANTED TO SEE WHY THIS SWIM HADN'T BEEN TURNING UP THE GOODS IN RECENT MATCHES. BACK TO THE POLE....

... THE ROACH ARE BACK SNAFFLING UP THE HEMP ON-THE-DROP.

DAMN! THE HOOK'S PULLED OUT AGAIN! THE FISH WAS JUST TOO POWERFUL FOR THIS DELICATE GEAR, BUT THE ACCELERATION TELLS ME IT'S CARP THAT ARE THE CULPRITS.

SEVEN TO EIGHT POUNDS OF SMALL CHUB DACE AND ROACH— DISAPPOINTING, BUT AN INDICATION HOW GOOD THIS VENUE IS COMPARED TO MANY CANALS.

NOVEMBER
Private Fenland Drains
Cambridgeshire

DR. BARRIE RICKARDS OF CAMBRIDGE UNIVERSITY TRAVELS THE WORLD AS ONE OF THE U.K'S TOP GEOLOGISTS, BUT HIS FIRST HOME IS THE CAMBRIDGESHIRE FENS WHERE HE HUNTS FOR PIKE AND ZANDER AT EVERY OPPORTUNITY. JUST AFTER FIRST LIGHT THIS MORNING, DAVE COSTER AND I MET UP WITH BARRIE ON A PRIVATE, NARROW DRAIN WHERE HE IS CONFIDENT OF SOME PIKE ACTION BEFORE 10 a.m.

BY 9 a.m. IT'S OBVIOUS THIS IS GOING TO BE A TOUGH DAY. BARRIE RECKONS THE REAL CULPRIT IS AN OVERNIGHT LOW PRESSURE FRONT WHICH MOVED QUICKLY ACROSS THE COUNTRY. THAT USUALLY SPELLS CURTAINS FOR BAIT FISHING IN ITS IMMEDIATE AFTERMATH, BUT LURES OFTEN PRODUCE UNDER THESE CONDITIONS SO HE RIGS UP HIS 5 ft AMERICAN BAITCASTING ROD WITH A MINI MULTIPLIER AND SHAKESPEARE BIG S PLUG. LAST WEEK HE HAD A 24 POUNDER ON THIS OUTFIT!

HERE'S JUST A SMALL SELECTION OF BARRIE'S LURES. THE SHAKESPEARE PLUGS INCLUDE THE BIG S AND RED AND SILVER POPPER. THERE ARE THREE VARIANTS OF THE NORWICH SPOON AND THE SPINNER SELECTION INCLUDES THE NEW KILKO WITH BLUE BARS. THE JOINTED PLUG ON THE LEFT IS A KWIKFISH K12. LURES MUST BE FISHED ON A COUPLE OF WIRE TRACES FOR SECURITY. SOMETIMES IT HELPS TO ADD A WYE LEAD AT THE HEAD OF THE TRACE WITH SPINNERS.

THE NEWS FROM DAVE'S SWIM ISN'T GOOD. HE HAS NETTED A SMALL RUDD BUT RECKONS HE'D BETTER GO HOME BEFORE HE CATCHES PNEUMONIA! AS HE TRUDGES OVER THE FIELDS TO HIS CAR, BARRIE LANDS ANOTHER JACK. BY LATE DECEMBER WHEN ALL THE WEED HAS DIED BACK, THERE'LL BE NO SIGN OF JACKS. ALL OF THEM WILL BE INSIDE MUCH BIGGER PIKE. SUDDENLY THE PUMP AT THE HEAD OF THE DRAIN STARTS UP — IT'S TIME TO GO.

WE THROW THE RODS IN THE BACK OF THE CAR AND SWITCH TO A KNOWN HOTSPOT FOR DOUBLES ON THE GREAT OUSE RELIEF CHANNEL. IT IS NOW 11 a.m. AND POURING WITH RAIN. THIS TIME BARRIE TRIES A MACKEREL TAIL AS WELL AS A SMELT. THE WIND THREATENS TO BLOW HIS RODS CLEAN OFF THE OPTONICS SO HE SECURES THEM WITH ELASTIC BANDS. HE STILL LIKES USING WASHING-UP BOTTLE TOPS TO SIGNAL DROP-BACKS AND INSERTS A STARLITE IN PLASTIC TUBING FOR SESSIONS AFTER DARK. WE SIT UNDER THE BROLLY FOR MORE THAN TWO HOURS WITHOUT A RUN. — THIS IS GETTING DESPERATE.

STARLITE

APPEARANCES ARE DECEPTIVE ON THESE TINY DRAINS. MANY OF THEM HOLD ENORMOUS STOCKS OF QUALITY BREAM AND ROACH WHICH GROW FAT IN THE ENRICHED WEEDY WATERS. PIKE ALSO PACK ON WEIGHT VERY QUICKLY AS THEY DON'T HAVE TO MOVE VERY FAR TO GRAB A SATISFYING SNACK, BUT YOU'VE GOT TO STAY OFF THE SKYLINE WHICH IS EASIER SAID THAN DONE ON THESE STEEP SIDED BANKS. BARRIE HAS DUG OUT A COUPLE OF SWIMS AND SETTLES INTO A FAVOURITE SPOT WHERE THERE'S 6FT OF WATER IN MID-CHANNEL.

Terry Whittaker

BARRIE HAS JUST SIGNED UP AS A SHAKESPEARE CONSULTANT AND IMMEDIATELY BAGGED A COUPLE OF THEIR THREE-PIECE EQUALISER RODS FOR HIS DEADBAIT FISHING. THEY ARE 3lb TEST CURVE BEASTS BUT BARRIE RECKONS THEY'VE GOT A SMASHING ACTION. HIS REELS ARE OLD, TRUSTY MITCHELLS AND THE LINE IS 12lb PLATIL. HE'S FISHING TWO RODS — ONE LEGER AND THE OTHER FLOAT — WITH SMELT DEADBAITS. ALTHOUGH THERE IS STILL A LOT OF BOTTOM WEED, THE PIKE SHOULD SOON SNIFF OUT THESE STRONG SMELLING FISH NO MATTER HOW FESTOONED THEY GET.

MEANWHILE, DAVE HAS SET UP IN A RAKED SWIM ABOUT 40 YARDS AWAY BUT HE'S NOT A HAPPY MAN. HE IS SUFFERING FROM A SEVERE HEAD COLD AND STRONG WINDS SWEEPING ACROSS THE FENS ARE NOT DOING HIM ANY GOOD AT ALL. THERE WAS ALSO AN OMINOUS TEMPERATURE DROP OVERNIGHT WHICH HAS CHILLED THE WATER AND THERE SEEMS LITTLE CHANCE OF THE BREAM FEEDING TODAY. DAVE IMMEDIATELY GOES ON PUNCHED BREAD IN THE HOPE OF SOME ROACH BUT HIS SWIM IS UNRESPONSIVE.

BARRIE'S DEADBAIT RIG

BILLY LANE STOP KNOT

BEAD

SLIDING PILOT FLOAT

12lb PLATIL MAIN LINE

BEAD

SNAPLINK SWIVEL

SWIVEL

3/4 OZ BOMB

UPPER WIRE TRACE 10-12 in.

THE SAME TERMINAL SET-UP IS ALSO USED FOR LEGER RIGS — WITH THE BOMB SOMETIMES FIXED ON THE SNAPLINK.

SNAPLINK SWIVEL

SIZE 8 TREBLES

SLIDING RYDER HOOK

AFTER WORKING HIS WAY ALONG THE EDGE OF THE DRAIN FLICKING OUT THE PLUG IN FRONT OF HIM, BARRIE SWITCHES TO A BIG SPOON — THE RESULT IS A JACK PIKE WHICH ISN'T MUCH LONGER THAN THE LURE!

ANOTHER CHANGE OF SCENERY! AT 2 p.m. WE SHOOT OVER TO THE DELPH TO WORK LURES THROUGH A ONE MILE STRETCH WHICH IS ABSOLUTELY SOLID WITH PIKE. IF WE DON'T GET A DOUBLE HERE THEN IT'S OBVIOUS THE WHOLE OF THE FENS HAS TURNED OFF. THE RAIN IS DRIVING INTO OUR FACES BUT WE RESOLUTELY FLASH AN ASSORTMENT OF SPOONS AND PLUGS THROUGH EVERY YARD OF WATER.

THAT'S THE NEAREST WE'VE COME TODAY! A FISH OF AROUND 8 lb FOLLOWS BARRIE'S SPOON ALL THE WAY TO THE BANK ONLY TO TURN AWAY AT THE LAST SECOND. IT WAS THE ONLY SIGN OF LIFE IN THE STRETCH. WE'RE BOTH SOAKED BUT WE'RE NOT BEATEN YET.

OUR LAST HOPE IS ANOTHER TINY DRAIN WHERE THE PIKE ARE USUALLY SUCKERS FOR A FLASHY SPOON. YOU'VE GOT TO ADMIRE BARRIE'S PERSISTENCE ON A DAY WHEN THE ODDS ARE TOTALLY STACKED AGAINST HIM. AT 4.30 p.m. WE ADMIT DEFEAT JUST AS THE SKIES CLEAR FOR THE FIRST TIME. THE WEAK WINTERY SUN RAISES OUR SPIRITS AND REMINDS US THAT TOMORROW COULD BE AS DIFFERENT AGAIN.

NOVEMBER
Stanborough Lake
Welwyn Garden City, Hertfordshire

THE WIND'S BLOWING UP A GALE TODAY LADS — LET'S GET THE DRAW OVER BEFORE THE RAIN STARTS.

TODAY'S OPEN AT STANBOROUGH LAKE SHOULD PRODUCE DOUBLE-FIGURE CATCHES OF ROACH AND BREAM. THERE'S ALSO THE CHANCE OF A GIANT PERCH. I'M JOINED AT THE DRAW BY MY TEAM-MATE GRAHAM SMITH.

HALF AN HOUR AND THERE'S MY FIRST BITE! FEELS LIKE A SKIMMER HAS PICKED UP MY RED MAGGOT HOOKBAIT.

GRAHAM HAS STARTED WELL ON THE 10 METRE POLE, PUTTING TOGETHER A STRING OF NICE ROACH — NOW HIS POLE ELASTIC IS REALLY STRETCHING AS HE PLAYS A BIG FISH.

I'VE GOT THE END RIG WORKING WELL NOW — BITES ARE COMING ON-THE-DROP.

THE POOR ANGLERS ON THE BANK TO MY RIGHT ARE HAVING ALL SORTS OF PROBLEMS.

THE POLE DIDN'T PRODUCE A BITE, ALTHOUGH TO BE FAIR I DIDN'T GIVE IT LONG. BACK TO THE OPEN-END FEEDER AND THE REST HAS DONE SOME GOOD — A NICE SKIMMER.

IV'E ONLY SET UP A LIGHT FEEDER RIG AND A SHORT POLE. THE WIND IS NEARING STORM FORCE. ANY OTHER METHODS ARE GOING TO BE IMPOSSIBLE TO CONTROL. I'VE STARTED ON THE FEEDER WHILE I TRY TO BUILD UP THE INSIDE POLE LINE.

GRAHAM SMITH

I'M USING A TARGET BOARD WITH A QUIVERTIP. IT'S GOING TO BE HARD ENOUGH TO SPOT BITES IN THIS DREADFUL WIND AND THE BOARD MIGHT JUST MAKE THE DIFFERENCE.

I'M GOING TO LENGTHEN MY HOOKLENGTH AND SCALE DOWN TO A 22 HOOK WITH DOUBLE RED PINKIE. A DRIER MIX IN MY CAGE FEEDER WILL ALSO GET MORE CLOUD INTO THE SWIM.

TWO HOURS INTO THE MATCH AND I'M NOW TRYING THE SHORT POLE "TO HAND" STYLE, BUT EVEN THIS IS DIFFICULT IN THIS WIND.

GRAHAM'S JUST KEPT SMALL HELPINGS OF LOOSE MAGGOTS GOING IN — HE COULD BE INTO DOUBLE FIGURES NOW. FOR ME THOUGH IT'S BEEN A RIGHT GRUELLER — ONLY ABOUT 4lb OF SKIMMERS.

RESULTS
1st. GRAHAM SMITH (Tottenham) 13·6·0
2nd. MELVIN REEVES (Stevenage) 9·3·0
3rd. STEVE TYLER (Poplett) 9·2·0

NOVEMBER
Grand Union Canal
Watford, Hertfordshire

KEY TO LADY CAPELS HOTSPOTS

1. SWIM BELOW HUNTON BRIDGE LOCK. MATCH-WINNING PEG. HAS PRODUCED MANY 2lb ROACH, BREAM TO 6lb, CHUB TO 4lb.

2. SEWERAGE OUTLET. TENCH SHOW HERE IN SUMMER.

3. NARROWS ABOVE HUNTON BRIDGE WIDES. NO COVER ON FAR BANK BUT SUPERB SKIMMER HOLDING SPOT.

4. UPPER WIDES. HOLDS BIG ROACH, CARP, SKIMMERS AND ONE SHOAL OF BIG BREAM.

5. MOTORWAY BRIDGE. GOOD CHUB PEG, BUT A BIT HIT OR MISS.

6. DEAD WATER. THROWS UP ODD GOOD WEIGHTS OF CHUB AND BREAM. CARP TO 14lb LIVE HERE.

7. MOUTH OF BACKSTREAM. TOP CHUB AND ROACH SWIM.

8. SHALLOWS. OVERGROWN FAR BANK HOLDS BIG CHUB. QUALITY ROACH SHOW DOWN MIDDLE TO LONG POLE. FAVOURED DRAW.

9. LADY CAPELS WIDES. THE 5 PEGS HERE ARE EVERY MATCHMAN'S DREAM DRAW, CAPABLE OF TURNING UP BIG WEIGHTS OF CHUB, BREAM, ROACH, CARP.

10. SCHOOLHOUSE BEND. FAR BANK TREE COVER HOLDS LOTS OF CHUB AND CARP.

11. RUSH BED. FULL OF CARP AND CHUB. A HEARTBREAK — DIFFICULT TO GET FISH OUT.

12. WHITE BRIDGE. CANAL NARROWS. CHUB AND ROACH ALWAYS RESIDENT.

13. CATTLE DRINK. GREAT ROACH PEG.

14. BOOM. BEST CHUB SWIM ON VENUE. HAS WON MORE MATCHES THAN ANY OTHER SWIM.

15. DEAD POUND. GOOD DRAW WHEN CANAL IS CARRYING EXTRA WATER. TURNS UP CHUB, SKIMMERS, ROACH AND GUDGEON. SOMETIMES WINS WINTER MATCHES.

16. GUDGEON ALLEY. FULL OF GUDGEON AND MINNOWS. ONE SWIM HAS A BUSH ON FAR BANK. THIS ALWAYS HOLDS BIG CHUB AND IS OFTEN A WINNING DRAW.

I'VE EXPLORED AROUND THE FAR-BANK TREES AND ALONG THE WALL AT THE BOTTOM OF THE GARDENS, BUT ONLY SMALL TAPS FROM GUDGEON HAVE RESULTED. I'M BEGINNING TO FEED SMALL AMOUNTS OF HEMP AND CASTERS AT POINTS A AND B. I'LL FISH THE MIDDLE ON THE WAGGLER AND POINT B ON THE 10 METRE POLE.

A CLASSIC CAPELS ROACH, A MINT CONDITIONED 14oz FISH. IT GAVE A GOOD ACCOUNT OF ITSELF ON LIGHT GEAR TOO, BUT THE ELASTIC REDRESSED THE SITUATION. EVEN WITH SUCH A FINE LINE YOU DON'T FEEL WORRIED IF YOU CAN GET THE ELASTIC/LINE RATIO RIGHT.

THAT'S FUNNY. BITES HAVE CEASED. IT'S PROBABLY BECAUSE THE EARLY MIST IS CLEARING AND THE SUN'S PUSHING THROUGH.

PERHAPS THE FISH HAVE MOVED OUT. I'LL GIVE THE WAGGLER A TRY.

A CAREFUL APPROACH IS NEEDED HERE ALSO. I'VE SET THE RIG A GOOD 18in OVER-DEPTH — THIS MEANS OVER-CASTING AND RETRIEVING THE END TACKLE TO GET IT WORKING CORRECTLY.

I'M FISHING PEG 73 ON THE LADY CAPELS WIDES TODAY. IT'S A GOLDEN DRAW ON A MATCH. THERE ARE ONLY FIVE SWIMS ON THIS FAVOURED SECTION — IN SEVEN YEARS I'VE ONLY DRAWN HERE ONCE. LET'S SEE WHAT I'VE BEEN MISSING.

I'M STARTING OFF WITH A FEW EXPLORATORY CASTS TO THE FAR SIDE WITH A SMALL DRENNAN FEEDER FILLED WITH MAGGOTS. DOUBLE MAGGOT NORMALLY SORTS OUT A FEW CHUB.

MAIN BOAT CHANNEL

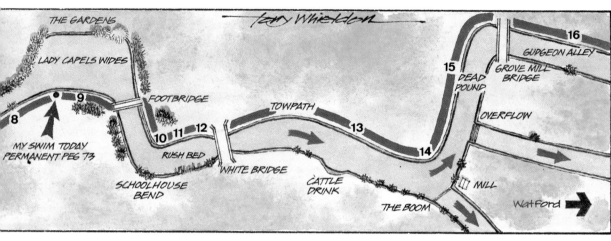

THE GARDENS

Tony Whieldon

LADY CAPELS WIDES

FOOTBRIDGE

8   9

MY SWIM TODAY PERMANENT PEG 73

10 11 12

RUSH BED

SCHOOLHOUSE BEND

WHITE BRIDGE

CATTLE DRINK

THE BOOM

TOWPATH

13

14

15   DEAD POUND

16

GUDGEON ALLEY

GROVE MILL BRIDGE

OVERFLOW

MILL

Watford →

LET'S GET THE POLE OUT. I THINK I'M DOING MORE HARM THAN GOOD WITH THE FEEDER, THE CANAL REALLY IS PAINFULLY CLEAR TODAY — OVERNIGHT FROST HAS KNOCKED THE COLOUR OUT.

I'VE SCALED MY TACKLE DOWN. I RECKON IT'S GOING TO BE HARD TO TEMPT A BITE! BECAUSE I'M USING SUCH A SMALL, FINE HOOK I'M NOT GOING TO HIDE THE HOOK IN THE CASTER — I'LL SIMPLY NICK THE END.

1 lb

4 x ·064g Styls

22 Blue Gamakatsu   5½ oz

THE FLOAT SHOT UNDER, BUT IT'S ONLY A TINY GUDGEON.

I HAD TO STEP UP THE FEED BECAUSE I WAS GETTING BITTED OUT BY GUDGEON AND MINNOWS. IT SEEMS TO HAVE WORKED, THIS FISH IS PULLING OUT AN EXTRA YARD OF MY POLE ELASTIC.

BECAUSE THE WATER'S STATIONARY 5 ROD LENGTHS OUT I'M HAVING TO USE A FLOATING LINE. I KEEP MENDING IT TO KEEP THE FLOAT STILL.

Slack

Current

THAT LITTLE BIT OF MOVEMENT ON THE END TACKLE, AS I MENDED THE LINE, TEMPTED A FAST BITE. *THIS IS BETTER!*

DAMN! THE FISH CAME OFF. IT MUST HAVE BEEN ONLY VERY LIGHTLY NICKED BY THE HOOK.

Grand Union Canal Continued

● If you like the look of Lady Capels, check before fishing that day tickets are still obtainable on the bank. Litter problems along this stretch became so bad that the controlling club issued a warning that day permits would be withdrawn unless there was an improvement. They were forced to act because the litter louts had jeopardised their long term control of the fishings.

WELL IT'S NO GOOD SITTING HERE NOT GETTING BITES. I'M GOING TO SCALE DOWN ON THE WAGGLER. I'VE BEEN FISHING A 1lb BOTTOM AND 18 FINE WIRE HOOK WITH MICRO SHOT DOWN THE RIG. LET'S TRY 12oz AND A 20 HOOK WITH 3 TINY STYL WEIGHTS SPREAD OUT.

1.5lb

Styl

Styl

Styl

12oz

Size 20 Fine Wire

I'VE GOT ONE GOOD ROACH IN THE NET AND BUMPED ANOTHER, BUT IT'S A REAL STRUGGLE IN THE BRIGHT SUN, WITH THE CANAL AS CLEAR AS TAP WATER.

ONE TRICK THAT OFTEN GETS YOU A BITE ON THESE TYPE OF DAYS IS TO KEEP TWITCHING YOUR FLOAT IN A FEW INCHES. THIS MOVES THE HOOKBAIT ALONG THE BOTTOM ....

....AND A FISH THAT'S BEEN A BIT UNSURE WILL OFTEN GRAB THE BAIT BY INSTINCT LIKE THIS ONE DID!

THREE GOOD ROACH, NOW I'VE HOOKED SOMETHING BIGGER. THIS ONE TOOK ON—THE—DROP.

I'VE REALLY GOT 'EM GOING NOW! WONDER WHAT THIS IS? IT IS'NT A CHUB, THE FIGHT IS TOO PONDEROUS.

A 1½lb BREAM. THIS IS TURNING INTO A NICE MIXED CATCH.

I TOOK ANOTHER BREAM ON THE WAGGLER AND THOUGHT I'D HAVE ONE MORE CHUCK IN ON THE POLE BEFORE I GO. I'M STRAIGHT INTO A BIG FISH.

THE MUCH LIGHTER STYL WEIGHTS AND MORE SUPPLE HOOKLENGTH GIVE A MUCH MORE NATURAL DESCENT TO THE HOOK-BAIT. I DON'T ADVOCATE GOING THIS LIGHT WHEN THERE ARE GOOD FISH AROUND, UNLESS YOU ARE SUPREMELY CONFIDENT OF YOUR TACKLE.

I KNOW MY WAGGLER ROD AND REEL CAN HANDLE SUCH FINE GEAR THAT SLOWER FALL FOOLED THIS FISH.

WHAT A LOVELY ROACH! A GOOD POUND FISH — AGAIN IN MINT CONDITION.

I REALLY ENJOY DAYS LIKE THIS. IT'S HARD, BUT I'M GETTING BITES BY CONSTANTLY CHASING AROUND THE SWIM — BUT I MISSED THAT ONE!

A 2lb PLUS CHUB.

THE LIGHT'S NOT QUITE SO BRIGHT NOW AND I'M GETTING A FEW MORE BITES. THIS IS A MUCH BIGGER FISH — IT'S TAKING A LOT OF LINE.

THREE MINUTES LATER.

A 4lb CHUB. IT'S SURPRISING HOW WELL 12oz LINE WILL STAND UP AGAINST A FISH LIKE THAT, BUT YOU MUST HAVE A ROD CAPABLE OF ABSORBING THE BUFFETING ACTIONS OF THE FISH.

AH! THAT'S A SHAME — AFTER SEVERAL MINUTES I WAS JUST STARTING TO MAKE AN IMPRESSION ON THE FISH WHEN THE TINY HOOK PULLED FREE. I SAW THE FISH, A GOOD CHUB OF OVER 3lb.

A TIDY CATCH FOR A FROST AFFECTED WINTER CANAL FISHERY. TWO CHUB, THREE ROACH AND TWO BREAM WITH A SMATTERING OF GUDGEON FOR DOUBLE FIGURES.

THE KINGS LANGLEY CLUB HAVE TURNED THIS FISHERY INTO SOMETHING A BIT SPECIAL. YOU CAN GET DAY TICKETS ON THE BANK AS LONG AS THE WATER ISN'T BOOKED.

NOVEMBER
Somerley Lakes
Ringwood, Hampshire

THE DAY TICKET SOMERLEY LAKES IN HAMPSHIRE CONTAIN SPECIMENS OF MANY SPECIES BUT ARE BEST KNOWN FOR THEIR CARP. ANDY LITTLE HAS JOINED ME TO EXPLORE THIS DEEP BAY WHERE A 30lb FULLY SCALED MIRROR IS BELIEVED TO BE RESIDENT. IT'S POSSIBLY THE BIGGEST FISH OF ITS KIND IN THE COUNTRY BUT HASN'T BEEN CAUGHT FOR SOME TIME.

MAGGOTS

MOST CARP ANGLERS AT SOMERLEY BELT THEIR BAITS INTO THE MIDDLE OF THE LAKE. ANDY'S DOING THE VERY REVERSE — HE'S CASTING HIS RIGS TIGHT INTO OVERHANGING BUSHES JUST A FEW FEET OUT.

BOILIE

THE BALANCED BOILIE ONLY JUST SINKS. EVEN WHEN IT FINALLY RESTS ON THE BOTTOM IT WILL RISE AGAIN IF IT'S DISTURBED BY A FISH.

ANDY'S GETTING LOTS OF TWITCHES ON THE MAGGOT RIG WHICH NEVER SEEM TO DEVELOP INTO A FULL-BLOODED BITE. HE HANGS A MINI BOILIE ON THE LINE IN AN EFFORT TO SHOW THE INDICATIONS MORE CLEARLY.

HE'S IN CONTROL NOW.

A LOVELY 17lb 12oz MIRROR

ON 10½ METRES I'VE FOUND A NICE SHELF GOING DOWN TO 8 Ft. THERE'S ABOUT 5 Ft JUST OFF THAT ISLAND. I'LL CATAPULT A FEW MAGGOTS ON EACH LINE EVERY NOW AND THEN AND SWITCH ABOUT UNTIL I CATCH.

POLE LINE

WAGGLER LINE

ISLAND

BALANCED BOILIE RIG

WATER REPELLENT FOAM INSERTED INTO DRILLED HOLE

FREE SWIMMING MAGGOT RIG

WATER RESISTANT FOAM 'MAGGOT'

AS FOR ME — I CAN'T TEMPT A BITE. I'VE EVEN TWITCHED MAGGOTS AND CHOPPED WORMS ALONG THE BOTTOM. THE BIG PERCH, ROACH AND CRUCIANS HAVE OBVIOUSLY BEEN TURNED OFF BY LAST NIGHT'S SEVERE FROST. I CAN SEE THE ODD ROACH TOPPING OVER IN THAT BAY — THINK I'LL MOVE TO THEM.

SUDDENLY ANDY GETS A SAVAGE TAKE ON HIS MAPLE BOILIE RIG. HIS CRAFTY PRESENTATION HAS OBVIOUSLY DONE THE TRICK.

THE FISH DIVES DEEP BELOW THE BUSHES BUT ANDY SUBMERGES HIS ROD UNTIL ONLY THE HANDLE IS SHOWING. IT ALLOWS HIM TO HEAVE THE CARP BACK WITHOUT THE LINE FOULING ANY TRAILING BRANCHES.

A LOT OF ANGLERS DRY NET ON DAYS LIKE THIS BY SITTING IT OUT. I HAD TO CHANGE SWIMS THREE TIMES TO LOCATE THE FISH. NOW I'M GETTING PLENTY OF BITES FROM SMALL ROACH.

ANDY'S HOPES OF HOOKING THE 30 POUNDER ARE FIRED BY HIS SUCCESS AND AT 2 p.m. HE GETS ANOTHER SCREAMING RUN ON THE BOILIE, BUT THE ACTION IS SHORT LIVED. THE HOOK BOUNCES OUT FROM A HARD PART OF THE MOUTH AND THE CARP CHARGES FREE.

IT WAS A PARTICULARLY TOUGH OFF-SET PATTERN OF HOOK BUT IT FINISHED UP WITH THE POINT SEVERELY DEFLECTED — JUST GOES TO SHOW THE POWER OF THESE FISH.

A DISAPPOINTING DAY FOR ME. I ENDED WITH 15 ROACH TO ½ lb. THE BIG ROACH AND PERCH DIDN'T SHOW. ANDY WAS JUSTIFIABLY PLEASED WITH HIS OWN FISH ALTHOUGH HE REALLY ONLY HAD EYES FOR THAT GIANT FULLY SCALED.

DECEMBER
Hampshire Avon
near Christchurch

THE SPOT I'VE CHOSEN HAS BEEN DICTATED BY THE ALMOST IMPOSSIBLE CONDITIONS. IT'S NOT THE MOST OBVIOUS SWIM FOR THE EXPECTED SPECIES HERE, CHUB AND BARBEL.

BUT I'VE FOUND A SMALL GRAVEL RUN THIS SIDE OF THE MIDDLE. MY FINE APPROACH AND REGULAR LOOSE FEEDING METHODS SHOULD EVENTUALLY DRAW SOME FISH IN.

WIND AND RAIN

EDDY

5FT

6FT

4FT

SHALLOWS

GRAVEL RUN

SHALLOWS

FRED'S USING HIS TRUSTED SPLIT-CANE ROD AND CENTREPIN REEL.
IT'S INTERESTING THAT HE DOESN'T PUT LASHINGS OF FEED DOWN AND ALSO TENDS TO SELECT SWIMS MANY ANGLERS WOULD IGNORE.

FRED'S METHODS

FRED HAS CAUGHT 170 BARBEL THIS SEASON, HIS BIGGEST CAME FROM THIS VENUE AND WEIGHED OVER 9lb.
RIGS 1-3 ARE USED IN HIS MAIN SWIM. RIG 4 IS FOR ROVING AND SEARCHING OUT ODD BIG BARBEL.

NEARLY 4lb, THAT FISH. A NICE START! IT GAVE A VERY FINICKY BITE THOUGH, EVEN ON A 1·7lb HOOKLENGTH AND 18 HOOK. I'LL KEEP REGULAR HELPINGS OF HEMP AND CASTER GOING IN AND TRY SINGLE CASTER ON THE HOOK.

I'M EXPERIMENTING WITH A NEW RIG. MY BULK SHOT IS A LONG STRING OF Nº 8s. MICHEL CUREAU, THE FRENCH INTERNATIONAL, SHOTS ALL HIS POLE RIGS IN SIMILAR FASHION. THOUGHT I'D TRY A HEAVIER VERSION ON RUNNING LINE.

SMALL ALL BALSA FLOAT

2·6lb

Nº 8s

1·7lb   Nº 8

Nº 10

18 BARBLESS

Nº 8s   Nº 4s

SMALLER SHOTS WITH SMALL GAPS BETWEEN OFFER LESS RESISTANCE AGAINST THE FLOW THAN LARGER ONES.

I MUST BE MAD TO BE OUT ON A DAY LIKE THIS! I'M ON THE LOWER AVON ABOVE CHRISTCHURCH AND THE CONDITIONS ARE AWFUL. THE RIVER'S LOWER THAN IT WAS DURING THE 1976 DROUGHT, IT'S BLOWING A GALE AND POURING WITH RAIN.

BIG BARBEL EXPERT FRED CROUCH IS FISHING UPSTREAM, BUT HE CAN'T TRY HIS FIRST CHOICE SWIM WHICH WOULD PUT HIM RIGHT IN THE TEETH OF THE GALE. HE'S SETTLED FOR A SPOT BY A FLOATING WEED RAFT. THIS SHOULD HOLD A FISH OR TWO IN THE LOW, CLEAR RIVER.

FRED PUTS SEVERAL DROPPERS OF HEMP, CASTERS AND MAGGOTS DOWN BY THE WEED. HIS SWIM IS 6ft DEEP. HE'S NOT OVER-CONFIDENT TODAY—THE WATER TEMPERATURE IS ONLY 44°F AND REGULAR READERS WILL KNOW HE BLANKED THE LAST TIME HE FISHED WITH ME.

HIS OWN DESIGN

BAIT·DROPPER

① Several to begin with

SWIMFEEDER

② Top up now and then

BOMB OVER BAITED AREA

③

④ Luncheon meat

Swan shot link

AFTER FLOGGING AWAY ON AN ALL BALSA RIG FOR AN HOUR, I'VE HIT INTO A GOOD CHUB ON DOUBLE CASTER.

IT WORKS WELL. IT'S POSSIBLE TO FISH A MUCH LIGHTER RIG, POSSIBLY HALF THE WEIGHT THAN IF USING LARGER SHOT.

HERE'S ANOTHER GOOD FISH!

Hampshire Avon Continued

● Fred Crouch is a rare breed of angler – he has concentrated exclusively on barbel for more than 30 years. He is famous for crossing swords with those who claim barbel in the late teens of pounds are there for the taking. According to Fred, giant barbel are very thin on the ground – and many of the monster sightings are mythical.

A BIT OVER 3lb, THIS ONE I'D SAY.

I'VE JUST HOOKED MY SECOND AVON FISH OF THE SESSION — ANOTHER NICE CHUB. THE WIND'S SO VICIOUS NOW I'M HAVING TO HOLD ON TO MY BROLLY AT TIMES.

I HAD SMALL TWITCHES ON THE QUIVERTIP IMMEDIATELY I CHANGED OVER TO THE BOMB. THE BITES AREN'T DEVELOPING THOUGH — MISSED THAT ONE.

I DON'T THINK THE TWITCH BITES ARE SMALL FISH — I'D HAVE HOOKED ONE BY NOW.

I'VE HAD THIS FISH ON FOR 10 MINUTES NOW, AND I'VE HAD TO LEAVE THE COMFORT OF MY BROLLY, AS IT GOT SIDEWAYS ON IN THE CURRENT AND THREATENED TO MOVE INTO THE SHALLOWS ROUND TO MY LEFT. IT'S OBVIOUSLY A NICE BARBEL.

BY NOT USING TOO POWERFUL A ROD I'VE MANAGED TO TURN THE FISH INTO THE SHALLOWS. IT'S AMAZING THE PRESSURE YOU CAN APPLY TO LIGHT LINES IF THE ROD MATCHES —NEARLY THERE.

FRED CROUCH IS STILL TUCKED AWAY UNDER HIS BROLLY TOO. SO FAR HE'S ONLY HAD ONE MISSED BITE.

MY SWIM HAS GONE DEAD ON THE FLOAT. LET'S TRY PUTTING A FEW FEEDER LOADS OF HEMP AND CASTERS OUT. I'VE BEEN LOOSEFEEDING BUT I'M NOT SURE HOW MUCH IS STAYING IN THE SWIM.

FLOW

LOOSE FEED HAS BEEN GOING IN HERE.

LANDING ON BOTTOM HERE

FEED TRUNDLING ALONG BOTTOM

B

SHALLOWS

I'VE DEPOSITED SEVERAL FEEDER LOADS AT POINT B. NOW I THINK I'LL SWITCH TO A BOMB LINK. IT'S A BIT LOW AND CLEAR TO KEEP CRASHING OUT THE FEEDER.

4·4lb BAYER

TWISTED NYLON LINK

KNOT

LOOP ATTACHMENT

LINK SWIVEL

2·6lb BAYER

¼oz BOMB

18 DRENNAN SPECIALIST

A REALLY POSITIVE TAKE AT LAST — THE QUIVERTIP PULLED FORWARDS AND DROPPED BACK VIOLENTLY. THOSE SMALLER INDICATIONS MUST HAVE BEEN LINERS FROM A BIG FISH. THIS IS REALLY POWERFUL.

RATHER THAN USE THE NET, I'VE GENTLY STEERED THE BARBEL ON TO THIS SANDY BEACH.

NOT BAD, THREE FISH FOR 14lb ON A DAY WHEN MOST METHODS WOULD BE DOOMED TO FAILURE. THE BARBEL WEIGHED 6lb 14oz, RATHER A LEAN FISH — IT LOOKED NEARER 8lb. THE CHUB WENT 3lb 12oz AND 3lb 6oz.
POOR FRED'S JINX CONTINUES, HE DIDN'T GET ANY ACTION. STILL HE'S NOT WORRIED, HE'LL SOON BE AMONGST THE FISH AGAIN. MY LIGHTER MATCH APPROACH MADE ALL THE DIFFERENCE TODAY. I MUST SAY WHEN YOU DO GET A FISH ON THE AVON IT'S A BIG'UN. THERE DON'T SEEM TO BE ANY SMALL FISH ABOUT — OR IF THERE ARE THEY MUST BE VERY LOCALISED. STRANGE, BECAUSE THE TYPE OF SWIM I FISHED WOULD NORMALLY HOLD PLENTY OF SMALL STUFF.

DECEMBER
Nottingham Embankment
River Trent, Nottinghamshire

I'VE DRIVEN UP THE MI IN THICK FOG FOR A DAYS FISHING WITH FELLOW MAIL COLUMNIST FRANK BARLOW. IT PROMISES TO BE A RIGHT LAUGH. FRANK'S GOT A TREMENDOUS SENSE OF HUMOUR, BUT HE'S EQUALLY FAMOUS IN THE MIDLANDS FOR HIS ABILITY WITH THE STICKFLOAT. WE'RE ON FRANK'S HOME TRENT WATERS AT NOTTINGHAM EMBANKMENT. HE LIVES JUST ACROSS THE RIVER WITH HIS LOVELY WIFE MO AND THREE SONS.

HE TELLS ME IT'S SOLID WITH FISH, BUT THERE'S JUST ONE SMALL SNAG — WE'VE PICKED A MONDAY. APPARENTLY THE TRENT ALWAYS SWITCHES OFF ON THIS DAY BECAUSE OF THE WAY THE POWER STATIONS OPERATE.

IS HE WINDING ME UP?

FISHING IS FREE FROM THE EMBANKMENT STEPS AND IT'S PERFECT STICK WATER. I'VE SET UP A LIGNUM STICK RIG, USING PAIRS OF Nº 8s FOR MY MAIN WEIGHTING. I CAN'T GET ON WITH BIGGER NON-TOXIC SHOT FOR THIS JOB. I'M EXPERIMENTING WITH A COUPLE OF STYL WEIGHTS AS DROPPERS.

Lignum stickfloat
Nº 8s
Nº 8s
Nº 8s
Nº 8s
1·5 lb
Nº 8s
Nº 10 styl
1 lb
Nº 10 styl

... A NICE ROACH OF ABOUT 14oz. FRANK'S BEEN JOINED BY HIS MATE BUTANE WHO HE SUSPECTS IS TRYING TO MUSCLE HIS WAY INTO THE DIARY. THE LEG-PULLING IS NOW IN FULL FLOW BUT I'M AFRAID WE CAN'T SAY THE SAME OF THE FISHING —
BITES ARE VERY SPASMODIC.

A COUPLE OF SMALL ROACH FOLLOW AND NOW HE'S HIT INTO SOMETHING BETTER....

MEANWHILE FRANK'S HOOKED A CHUB WHICH IS SOMETHING OF A RARITY FOR THESE PEGS.

I TOOK A COUPLE OF NICE ROACH AND BUMPED OUT OF A CHUB, BUT SPORT SUDDENLY DIED AWAY. FRANK SWITCHED TO THE WAGGLER, BUT APART FROM A FEW MORE ROACH HIS SWIM HAS DIED TOO. IT SEEMS THE RIVER NEEDS AN INFLUX OF RAIN WATER TO GET IT OUT OF THE DOLDRUMS.

FRANK'S RIG DIFFERS FROM MINE SLIGHTLY.

Original Pete Warren StickFloat (Frank says it's the last in his box and must not be lost otherwise there'll be big trouble)

2lb

Nº 8s

Nº 10

1lb   22 Mustad 90430

THE TRENT'S RUNNING CLEAR AFTER HEAVY FROSTS AND IT'S VERY SLOW AT THE START. MAYBE FRANK'S RIGHT ABOUT THE FISH GETTING MONDAY BLUES. WE'RE BOTH FEEDING BRONZE MAGGOTS STEADILY. FRANK'S BEGINNING TO WORK HIS WAY FURTHER OUT TO SEE IF HE CAN FIND SOME ACTION.

I'VE NOTICED HE HAS STRUNG HIS SHOTTING LOWER DOWN. I THINK HE'S DOING THIS TO USE WHAT FLOW THERE IS TO PULL HIS RIG THROUGH. HE'S USING A SHAKESPEARE PRESIDENT FLOAT ROD AND IT GIVES HIM COMPLETE CONTROL OVER HIS BLACK TIPPED STICK AS IT GLIDES DOWNRIVER. AFTER A FEW MISSED BITES FRANK GOES FURTHER OUT AND IS INTO A FISH.

AFTER SEEING FRANK CATCH BY GOING FURTHER OUT I'VE STEPPED UP MY FLOAT SIZE AND DONE THE SAME WITH AN IMMEDIATE RESPONSE.

I ENDED UP WITH THESE TWO NICE ROACH AND A FAIR SMATTERING OF BITS — POOR FOR THE TRENT, BUT IT'S BEEN A BIT ERRATIC THIS SEASON.

FRANK'S ENDED UP WITH 5—6 lb FOR A SECTION WIN AS HE PUTS IT.

WE MIGHT NOT HAVE BAGGED UP BUT IT'S BEEN A SMASHING DAY. FRANK'S A GREAT BLOKE AND WE'VE HAD A GOOD LAUGH. WE'RE OFF UP THE PUB FOR A CHRISTMAS PINT, OR TWO.

INDEX